The SCREAMING Stone

Radically Shaped by the Hand of God

Dr. James and Jana Chatham

The Screaming Stone

© 2014 by Dr. James and Jana Chatham

ISBN: 978-1-940084-03-9

All rights reserved. No part of this book may be reproduced or transmitted in any form or by any means, electronic or mechanical, including photocopying and recording, or by an information storage and retrieval system, without permission in writing from the authors.

Some of the anecdotal illustrations in this book are true to life and are included with permission of the person involved. All other illustrations are composites of real situations, and any resemblance to people living or dead is coincidental.

Creative team: Lorraine Pintus (book coach and editor); Rebecca Pearce (copy editor and proofreader); and Plaid Agency, George Meyer (cover design).

Unless otherwise noted, Scriptures are taken from the New American Standard Bible NASB®, Copyright© The Lockman Foundation 1960, 1962, 1963, 1971, 1972, 1973, 1975, 1977, 1995. Used by permission.

Scripture quotations marked NLT are taken from the Holy Bible, New Living Translation®. Copyright© 1996. Used by permission of Tyndale House Publishers, Inc., Wheaton, Illinois, 60189. All rights reserved.

Scripture quotations marked NIV are taken from the Holy Bible, New International Version®. Copyright© 2011. Used by permission of Biblica, Inc.® All rights reserved worldwide.

Scripture quotations marked ESV are taken from the Holy Bible, English Standard Version, Copyright© 2001 by Crossway Bibles, a division of Good News Publishers. Used by permission. All rights reserved.

1. Personal transformation through suffering—biblical perspective.
2. Grief. 3. Marriage.

Printed in the United States of America

To our oldest daughter, Julie Chatham Carroll for
her steadfast love of God and her love for us.

In loving memory of our youngest daughter, Jenny Lynn Chatham.

Contents

Acknowledgements 1
1 Even the Stones Cry Out. 3
2 Battered in the Streambed. 23
3 Glimmer in the Gravel 45
4 Birthmarks and Blemishes. 65
5 Never Let Go. 87
6 An Emerald, a Green Flash, and a Changed Life. 109
7 The Daily Grind 131
8 The Scream of Surrender 153
9 Absolute Surrender 171
10 Absolute Honor. 195
11 A Diamond Named Hope 213

Epilogue. 235
Chapter Questions. 241
Endnotes 253

Acknowledgements

We wish to acknowledge and thank our family and friends who stood beside us during the difficult years with Jenny, especially those weeks and months immediately following her death. In particular, we thank our former church family at Faith Christian Community, Anchorage, Alaska. Your attentive ear and validating words of encouragement were the crutches on which we staggered in our feeble attempts to carry on with life.

We also recognize those specific Alaska friends whose love and encouragement gave us the will to continue. We are especially indebted to Mark and Karen Barnett for their attentive care during many precious evenings together, the trip to Hawaii to scatter Jenny's ashes, and the recreational activities that provided desperately needed intermissions to the dark agony of grief. We also thank Rick and Carolyn Rios for their wise and steadfast counsel that encouraged us to share our inner pain and pen this book and for the generous use of their beach condo that served as a "writing getaway." We thank our daughter, Julie, and son-in-law, Jason, for life-giving joy, for the creative ways to remember Jenny, and for raising up the next godly generation. We thank Carol (Jim's sister) and Hal (Jana's brother) for their faithful prayers and deep conversations, as we struggled to reason and understand the events that engulfed us.

We are forever indebted to Jim and Janet Carroll for the many years of life we shared together, for their love of Jenny as a daughter, and for Jim's flight to Texas to stand beside me (Jim) during the darkest week of my life. We also thank Senior Pastor Steve and Deanna Holsinger for their counsel and for Steve's "red-eye" trip to Texas to deliver his tender memorial message. And, most recently, we are indebted to our California friends, Stacy and Peggy, and Scott and Sandi, for making us a part of their lives and for their loving encouragement to finish this book.

Finally, we graciously thank our dear friend and book coach, Lorraine Pintus, for her endless patience, wise counsel, and relentless insistence to "show and not tell." Her ruthless grammatical corrections to these Texans' scribbles made this book readable; her phenomenal encouragement helped us persevere through each page. Lorraine, you have been our loyal friend and counselor. You urged us to probe our deepest emotions and pen this book of healing—for our sake, and for the sake of many others.

CHAPTER 1

Even the Stones Cry Out

A SHARP, HIGH-PITCHED SCREAM interrupts our giggles, as the girls and I (Jana) recap the evening softball games. We pause and look towards the basement door. We'd tuned out the distant hum for the last twenty minutes—the sound of a motor intermingled with a soft, rhythmic pulse.

The scream stops. We continue laughing about Julie's botched slide into home plate that produced a fresh "raspberry" on her thigh and Jenny's splits into second base. Then...

Skreeeeech!

There it is again! Like the shriek of a cat with its tail caught under a rocking chair, the scream sends goose bumps up my arms. Those unfamiliar with the shriek would either run away in fear or run to the source to see who was in pain. But for me, the scream brings a burst of excitement and anticipation. I smile. I know.

Something wonderful is about to happen.

This scream, born of intense pressure, is a signal—a sign that something formerly rough is about to be transformed into something of exquisite beauty.

I tiptoe quietly down the basement stairs. In the corner I see Jim, my husband, hunched over a microwave-sized wood and metal box, a lapidary machine called a Facetron®. White light floods the area of his work space.

In his hand is the source of the scream—a gemstone in the final stage of polishing.

Strange. Before I married Jim I never believed it was possible for a stone to scream. But now that I understand the process Jim follows as he cuts gemstones, I know that in order for a stone to be transformed into a dazzling gem, it must scream.

First comes grinding. Then intense pressure. And then the scream. And after the scream? The grand finale of transformation—a brilliant gemstone.

Seven years later a different scream pierces our night.

JANA'S SCREAM

"Noooooooo!"

I dropped the phone on the bed and released the gut-wrenching scream of anguish from my soul.

It can't be true. This couldn't be happening.

But it was, and no amount of praying or wishing could transport me back moments earlier before the 4 a.m. phone call when my world fell apart. Mother's words replayed in my mind.

"It's Jenny. She's dead."

Dead? My Jenny... my daughter? My heart stopped.

"I found her... collapsed... on the floor." Mother's voice quivered, as she forced the words. "There was nothing I could do... I tried... coroner is here... they're taking her body. I'll call you back in a minute."

The click on the other end of the line had triggered my scream. It wasn't true—it *couldn't* be true. I'd talked with Jenny for over an hour on the phone last night. She was homesick. She cried and said she wanted to come home. She asked about Rudy and Rastis, her dogs. To cheer her up we'd chatted about college in the fall. She told me about her new apartment. She mentioned an itchy rash on her legs—I told her to take Benadryl®. What had she said before she'd hung up? What had been her last words? Could it be possible that I'd never hear her voice again?

Mother must be wrong, I told myself. *Jenny is nineteen and alive and well in Texas.* The phone rang. I grabbed it. Mother offered new information about the details of the morning that doused the tiny flame of hope I'd tried to kindle that Jenny was still alive. Apparently, the evening before, Jenny had taken several things to stop the itch, including alcohol and pills from some bottles that were on the bathroom countertop. The alcohol, combined with the pills—her bipolar prescriptions—and the Benadryl®, had formed a lethal combination.

Indeed, Jenny was dead.

Jim and I flew from our home in Alaska to Texas for the funeral. The trip was miserable. Nine days earlier I'd suffered a bad fall and had broken my ankle just as I was recovering from reconstructive shoulder surgery. A heavy cast confined my leg, which had to be elevated during the eight-hour flight. My leg throbbed with pain. The metal plate inserted during surgery encouraged healing of my fractured ankle, but I knew that no surgery could repair the bleeding gashes in my heart from losing Jenny.

I sat in my wheelchair at the memorial service and listened, as the pastor tried to make sense of what was incomprehensible. Nothing can prepare a parent for the soul-searing sorrow of losing a child—the one to whom you gave life, the one upon whom you pinned so many hopes and dreams. The steel frame of my wheelchair held my body upright, but inside, my soul had collapsed.

The days in Texas, and the ones that followed, after we returned home to Alaska, became an overgrown jungle of physical and emotional pain. I could not distinguish between the pain throbbing in my ankle and the relentless grief pounding in my chest. Because of my severe allergy to pain medication, I'd developed a high tolerance to pain at a young age. But this pain I could not tolerate. Every part of me screamed in agony—my ankle hurt, the screws in my shoulder throbbed. My thoughts hurt, my heart hurt, my soul ached. Pain filled every moment, as slowly, ever so slowly, moments ground into hours, hours into days, and days into weeks. To cope, I withdrew and isolated myself from people and anything connected to real life. I stopped attending Bible study, going to lunch with friends, even doing ordinary duties like paying bills. Everything seemed meaningless. Nothing mattered when compared to the earthshaking reality that Jenny was dead.

My dissociation protected me from the hurtful comments of others who had no clue how to deal with my raw grief. In isolation I learned to numb my emotions. In fact, I was so intent on numbing my pain that I often had to remind myself to breathe, but even breathing hurt.

Finally I'd coax my emotions into a state of numbness so I could function, but then something would happen to trigger the pain. I'd find a note Jenny had written, receive a letter in the mail addressed to her, or receive a phone call from another of Jenny's friends asking to speak to her, who didn't know of her death, only to be forced to comfort them. Pain released *again*. Again, the cycle would repeat. I'd withdraw inside myself and force my emotions to shut down. I couldn't face the pile of thank-you notes that needed to be written to people who had made donations in Jenny's memory or offered comfort to our family. Each note would be another acknowledgement that her death was real. This was the gut-wrenching grief cycle—fresh pain, numbness, fresh pain, numbness—my reality of life without Jenny.

On the rare occasion when I answered the telephone and allowed someone to invade my numb world, they'd ask, "How are you?" How was I? Ha! If people really knew, they'd lock me up and throw away the key! My thoughts bounced around like a ping pong ball on steroids. *I need to call Jenny about... Oh, wait. She's gone. No, she isn't. I can hear her voice from her phone message.* I played the voice recording at least a dozen times in those days following her death just to hear her sweet voice say, "Hey. This is Jenny. I'm out doing something better than talking on the phone. Leave your name and number and I'll get back at ya."

Two months after the funeral the doctor prescribed freedom from my wheelchair, but my newfound physical freedom provided little emotional freedom for my soul. Removal of my cast did not remove the hard shell I'd formed around my ravaged heart to protect it.

I'm tired, Lord... so weary. Stop the pain. It hurts so badly. Make it STOP.

Four months after Jenny's death, Jim left town on his first business trip since the funeral. His absence intensified my isolation and the darkness hovering over my heart. During the night, nightmares ruled. To cope, I stopped sleeping. Two or three days would pass until exhaustion took over and I'd pass out, only to be startled awake, terrified afresh by my new reality: Jenny was gone. Forever.

People encouraged me to get out, to do something outside the walls of my home. I forced myself to attend a church meeting, thinking it would be a good distraction from my pain. At the end of the meeting the leader asked for prayer requests. I took a huge risk and laid my heart on the line.

"Please pray for me. Jim is out of town and I'm not doing well. I miss Jenny so much, and I'm not able to sleep." Tears filled my eyes.

The group surrounded me and prayed. What happened next became another blur of pain. *I know they mean well, Lord, but their words cut deep.* "Stuck in grief?" "You should take sleeping pills." "You need to be on antidepressants." *Lord, if they only knew how much their words hurt. If only I could take a pill and get relief. People say they're watching me. I feel like I'm in a glass room screaming, and no one can hear my screams. I don't want them staring at my tears. Even my dearest friend says I've put up a steel wall to keep people away. And why shouldn't I? I know people mean well, but they say things that cut like a knife into my raw and bleeding heart.*

Several more days passed with little sleep. Darkness descended, thick and heavy. Suffocating. I couldn't breathe.

I'm tired, Lord...so weary. Stop the pain. It hurts so badly. Make it STOP. I repeated the words over and over, but the pain continued.

Okay, God, if You won't make the pain stop, I will!

I retrieved from the medicine cabinet multiple bottles of unused pain medicine from recent surgeries. Carefully I laid them out. One by one I caressed the top of each pill with my finger trying to sense their numbing power. I stared at the long line of pills on my desk. Is this enough? Yes, these would stop the pain. Darkness filled my home and heart. My devoted affection for my husband and our other daughter, Julie, wasn't enough to stifle the demonic thoughts that blackened my mind. *You're a mess. You're a failure as a wife and mom. Jim and Julie would be better off without you. You didn't help Jenny on her last night; you told her to just go take a pill. Maybe that's what killed her. Just end your life now. You don't deserve to live. Besides, death will stop the pain.*

Before I could ingest the miniature pharmacy, I looked upward and inwardly screamed, "God, help me!"

Softly, God instructed my heart. "Turn *to* the Light...turn *on* the light."

"Yes, Lord." I said out loud. I hobbled around the house and began to flip on lights. Bedroom lights. Closet lights. Lamps in the family room. The light above the stove. The light *in* the stove. I couldn't locate lights fast enough or turn them on quickly enough. It seemed that with each click of the switch, another small ray of hope illuminated the darkness in my soul. When my surroundings were as bright as they could possibly be, I grabbed my Bible and put it on my desk beside the pills. It fell open to Psalm 139. My eyes locked onto the page, and the words reached out and grabbed my heart:

> I could ask the darkness to hide me and the light around me to become night—but even in darkness I cannot hide from you. To you the night shines as bright as day.
> (Psalm 139:11, 12a, NLT)

God, I've tried to hide in the darkness alone to escape the pain, but that only made things worse. I need You. Are You here?

Then a soft, almost undetectable breeze—a breath of air—waltzed through the room. The stir of air and the glow of the lights stilled my racing thoughts. *Yes, You are with me...thank You.* It was as if the physical light around me had become spiritual light inside me. His love flooded every dark crevice, vanquishing the suicidal thoughts that had urged me to take my life. The rest of the night, I hobbled around my home, walking in the light and reading aloud words from *the book of Light,* the Bible. Scripture poured out a comforting balm over my bleeding wounds. Over the months that followed, slowly, ever so slowly, my silent screams turned into something else altogether—a whisper of praise of how God had saved my life and restored to me a glimmer of hope that, even though Jenny was gone, life could go on.

JIM'S SCREAM

Jana and I slept soundly on a mattress on the floor of our small townhouse subbasement, still in transition from a recent move with furniture in storage. The move had perpetuated the chaos in our lives, yet we dared to hope that a more stable environment lay just around the corner.

Brrrring!

The 4 a.m. phone call aroused me from a deep sleep. Jana fumbled for the phone and muttered a "hullo." My mother-in-law's quivering voice commanded Jana, "Get Jim on the phone with you."

Jana held the receiver between us so we could both listen. Whatever her mother had to say could not be good, not with this formality at this hour.

Her words bludgeoned me like an airborne sack of concrete. "Jenny is dead."

"Noooooooo!" Jana's scream ripped through the house at the news. After her mother hung up, we sat on the mattress, stunned. A crushing blackness crept over me and pressed upon my heart. Even my hands seemed unbearably heavy. Unsuspectingly, a wretched thought slithered into my mind: *Now you never have to worry about Jenny and her finances again.* Where had that thought come from? Yes, my conversation last week on the phone with Jenny had been difficult and tense, as we'd discussed her financial situation; still, how could I even think such a thing at a time like this? What kind of father was I?

Jana and I tried to imagine Jenny's final moments. Had she cried out for either of us? For God? The clock dropped another minute, but for us, time had frozen. How could life possibly go on without Jenny?

Dozens of scenes flashed through my dazed mind. Jenny and I bouncing each other on the family trampoline. Salmon fishing on the Kenai River. Teaching her how to change her car tires. Our last hike. She and I camping together on the beautiful, frigid Russian River. Could it be true? We were best of "buds." Would there never be another memory made together?

Another barbed accusation pierced my mind: *Jana and Jenny spoke together for over an hour last night on the phone. You were too busy mowing the grass to even say hello. Some father you are. Now you'll never speak to her again!*

Tears flowed. We slumped together on the rumpled sheets. I pulled Jana close. As we clung together in the cold, predawn darkness Rudy, our golden retriever, and Rastis, our terrier, climbed on to the mattress and lay against us, as if they understood what had just happened. *Can they know? Do they, like me, need the touch of human flesh at such a time as this?* Their warm, furry coats offered small patches of solace against the dark, chilly room. Rudy, the ever-loyal companion, nuzzled his damp, warm nose under my hand and flipped it upward to receive a caressing stroke on his forehead. *Jenny would have giggled at his demand for attention. Oh Jenny, Jenny... how could this happen?*

"Your mother mentioned pills. Do you think it could have been...suicide?" I asked, dreading Jana's reply.

"Mother said the coroner didn't suspect suicide, but I just don't know," Jana sobbed.

Our last five years with Jenny had been a nightmare. A dark, rebellious streak emerged that displaced her former, fun-loving nature. She disobeyed our counsel. She defied curfews and house rules. She developed addictions and an eating disorder. Eventually the doctors diagnosed her with bipolar disorder. Three months earlier she'd returned to her second treatment center, a residential center in Texas. The powerful medications and therapy had helped stabilize her, and she seemed happier. She enjoyed her two part-time jobs. I was scheduled to visit her in two weeks to go car shopping. Jenny said she'd changed—that she was actively seeking God after rejecting Him for four years—but I wondered. *Father, had she fully surrendered her life to You?*

The uncertainty sickened me.

"We have to pray," I urged Jana.

We clutched each other in the inky darkness and cried out to God for comfort—for simple breath to make it through the next few hours. We prayed for wisdom with the myriad of arrangements that now loomed before us: Purchase plane tickets to Texas, plan a memorial service, notify relatives, find someone to watch the dogs while we were away. We asked for strength just to crawl off the sheets and stand up—not a simple act with Jana's leg in a cast.

But even as my feeble prayers of helplessness ascended from deep within a broken heart, endless questions pummeled my mind. Surely this hadn't taken God by surprise. Had He been with Jenny during her final hours? What was her spiritual destination? Was she in heaven? If Jenny was with God, I yearned to pray to the Lord and ask Him to tell her how dearly we loved her, how proud we were of her. *But can you pray for the dead? Oh God! I'm so confused.*

As Jenny's father, I loved to help her. I helped her with endless hours of math homework. I helped her and her dear friend, Jessie, build "kamikaze" go-carts. I helped her find the newborn moose calf, whose mother angrily chased us and Rudy back into our house. I carried her home after her first arrest for "driving under the influence" and tried to help her understand the folly of her choices. And I tried to help her during her lonely days in the treatment centers by patiently listening to her inner struggles. But when she needed me most of all—only four hours earlier—where was I? I failed to help her then, and I was just as helpless now.

No more words... not another thought to pray... nothing but a dark numbness that seeped through my weakened soul. And then, in that vulnerable state another horrible accusation assaulted my mind: *Jenny wanted to come home and see you. You told her no. You said she needed to stay in treatment. Now she's dead. She died alone. A great protector you are! You don't even know where she is!*

Noooooooo!

An internal scream ripped through the deepest recesses of my soul.

Jenny was gone. Jenny, my little girl. No amount of praying or pleading or weeping could ever bring her back.

A GEMSTONE IN THE MAKING

Jenny's death plunged us both into a dizzying whirlpool of guilt and second guesses. We floundered in suffocating currents of painful memories and self-condemnation. Waves of anguish pounded us so intensely we doubted we'd survive and, at times, we didn't even care to.

But *we did* survive.

God taught us new things to do together as a couple, and He reinforced the former things that comforted us individually. For example, one thing that comforted me (Jim) was the process of cutting gemstones. I knew I could never restore Jenny's life, nor could I stop the waves of anguish, but I could dampen the pain by cutting a stone.

Beautiful memories of both my girls, Julie and Jenny, at the lapidary desk, would flood my mind as I fashioned each gem. We'd cut stones together when they were younger. And we'd marvelled together at the brilliant splendor of transformation—how a dull, rough stone could become a gorgeous, sparkling gem. As I sat at my desk bathed in the glow of white light, I found myself strangely soothed by these precious memories, by the methodical process of cutting and polishing, and by the coveted anticipation of the beauty of transformation.

In the pages of this book we'd like to share how it's possible to be changed from dull to dazzling and how God can take a scream of pain and turn it into a cry of praise. We'll do this by sharing with you the physical process of cutting a gemstone and applying some of the amazing spiritual parallels we discovered that brought healing to our ravaged souls. As we do, we pray that the light of the lapidary desk and the light of His truth will bless you.

Quartz is the second-most common mineral on the planet. It often makes up over 50% of the sand grains on a common beach. You've probably seen the beautiful, glassy-clear crystals in rock shops—these are quartz in its purest form. When tainted by tiny concentrations of other chemicals during its growth as a crystal, it takes on various colors. The royal purple (amethyst) and deep yellow (citrine) varieties are commonly cut as gemstones.

Ametrine is a spectacular combination of amethyst and citrine in the same crystal. It is found only in the Anahi mine in eastern Bolivia, South America. The six-sided crystals range from four inches to a foot in length and two to five inches in diameter. Curiously, instead of the colors simply blending together, each side of the six-sided crystal alternates between amethyst and citrine.

The crystals are often broken during mining. The chunks of "rough" that are sold as gem-quality material include both amethyst and citrine that join along a flat, razor-thin plane. The gemstones are cut with a purple and yellow side divided along the center of the stone.

THE MUSINGS OF A LAPIDARY

In my hand I hold a piece of "rough," a former crystal of ametrine thirty carats in weight. This particular type of stone has qualities that we cherish. Two distinct colors—royal purple amethyst and canary yellow citrine—saturate separate portions of the same stone.

Examine the stone with me. Fractured, dull, and poorly shaped, and similar to a frosted piece of glass, yet notice the subtle glow beneath the rough exterior, as light from the overhead lamp penetrates the stone. Can you see it? Can you see the hint of stunning beauty concealed within?

As the lapidary, my goal is to release the beauty of this stone. I study it carefully until I know it intimately—every undulation and blemish on its rough exterior.

Next, I flip down my magnifying visor and peer into the stone's interior. Life's events have shaped and marred this stone from its origin as a unique and beautiful crystal in a rock matrix. Each imperfection I see speaks of a very personal journey. No other stone has this gem's qualities nor its individual fractures and flaws. These scripts define the stone's personal story and influence the design I will choose for it. After studying the stone, I determine that the best design to release its beauty will be a rectangular step-cut.

Cutting a stone is a tricky process. If I overcut and grind too deeply, I lose some of the stone's precious material. If I undercut, I leave behind fractures or blemishes that hinder the reflection of light. I will do everything in my power and training to unveil the brilliance of this stone, but it must be handled tenderly and with great attention to the individual nuances that make it unique from all others. I'll use the fiery pressure of polishing as the final step to unleash the stone's full brilliance.

I'm guessing that, by now, you already suspect some of the spiritual principles that emerge from this process. For example, just as I am a human lapidary who cuts and polishes physical stones, God is the Master Lapidary who cuts and polishes us, His "living stones."[1] And, just as I peer into the stone to find the flaws and inclusions, God also looks deeply into our hearts and sees our fractured lives and impurities. He notes the blemishes of selfishness and pride that must be removed. He examines us and determines the plan that will bring forth beauty and brilliance.

As you journey through this book, I'll carry you through each step of the process, as we cut and polish this ametrine and watch its transformation into a sparkling gem. We'll share with you many spiritual analogies.

This book is about stones—stones birthed from the earth as well as living stones birthed by the Spirit of God. And it's about transformation. God transforms us one facet at a time, just like the stones I shape, so we might reflect His glory.

Paul writes beautifully about this process:

> But we all, with unveiled face, beholding as in a mirror the glory of the Lord, are *being transformed into the same image from glory to glory*, just as from the Lord, the Spirit.
> (2 Corinthians 3:18, emphasis ours)

To move from glory to glory is a heavenly change we can only imagine. To be transformed from sinful humans into the image of Christ—this is unfathomable beauty beyond the finest gem and something we desperately need.

But how does God apply His "lapidary skills" to transform us? Press on.

THE ESSENCE OF TRANSFORMATION

Whether you're a "senior" Christian, a newborn Christian, or maybe you're not a Christian, you probably agree philosophically that being changed into a better human being is a worthy goal, especially if you more closely resemble Jesus. However, we must be honest about the process: It's difficult, it hurts, and "it ain't fun!" But we're convinced that the pain is worth it, as we're drawn to a closer, sweeter relationship with God than we can dare to imagine.

Transformation is a lifelong process that replaces our self-absorbed nature with a life fully surrendered and dependent upon God. Only then can our life reflect His love and light. As a couple, we've learned that God will often use our darkest trial as the roots of our deepest transformation. John Piper stated it well:

No one ever said that they learned their deepest lessons of life, or had their sweetest encounters with God, on the sunny days. People go deep with God when the drought comes. That is the way God designed it. Christ aims to be magnified in life most clearly by the way we experience Him in our losses.[2]

How about you? You may never have lost a child, but you've experienced other losses. How have you suffered? Maybe you've lost a job, your marriage, or the home you loved. Or maybe your health is your concern. Or perhaps you've watched a lifelong dream shatter before your eyes. Do you believe God can take each extremely painful situation, even your most grievous loss, and reveal glory through it?

Truthfully, most of us desire the end result—an intimate relationship with God that reflects His glory—but we'd sure prefer to avoid the pain in the process. That's why, in the midst of our pain, we must remember that God works *through* our pain to change us into something beyond all we dare to ask or dream.[3]

We've experienced several benefits of transformation in the process of healing from Jenny's death. We'll elaborate more on these throughout this book, but we've listed five concepts below that have proven true for us. We offer them with the prayer that they might prove useful to you as well.

Transformation hurts, but it removes our sin. Just as I, the human lapidary, polish away the flaws of a stone, God polishes away our impurities through suffering. First Peter 4:1 and 2 (NLT) says that Christ suffered in His body and that we should copy Him because "...if you have suffered physically for Christ, you have finished with sin. And you won't spend the rest of your life chasing after evil desires, but you will be anxious to do the will of God."

Transformation hurts, but it teaches us to trust God. The Apostle Paul may never have suffered your specific tragedy, but he experienced shipwrecks, physical beatings, starvation, and public ridicule. He vehemently states that his suffering was not in vain but for a valuable purpose: "...this happened that we might not rely on ourselves but on God..." (2 Corinthians 1:9).

Transformation hurts, but our pain can comfort others. Those who suffer learn a new language, a mysterious language infused with consoling words and phrases that transfers comfort to others going through similar trials. As a result, we are to praise God, "[who] comforts us in all our troubles so that we can comfort others. When others are troubled, we will be able to give them the same comfort God has given us" (2 Corinthians 1:4, 5, NLT).

Transformation hurts, but it produces godly character. Romans 5:3-5 tells us to "exult [rejoice] in our tribulations, knowing that tribulation brings about perseverance; and perseverance, proven character; and proven character, hope." The passage emphasizes we exult in hope because "hope does not disappoint."

Transformation hurts, but it increases our value. The cost per carat of a finely cut sapphire or tanzanite may exceed that of the rough stone by fifteen-fold. Likewise, as God cuts away our flaws, our value increases because it reveals a deeper faith. According to 1 Peter 1:7, a faith built through suffering is "more precious than gold" and will "result in praise, glory and honor" to God.

Transformation, then, brings a *powerful good* to our lives. It purifies us from sin, enables us to comfort others, teaches us to trust God, shapes our character, and enhances our value.

As I (Jim) consider the ametrine in my hand and understand what I must do to transform this piece of rough into a gemstone ready for display, I'm humbled by the process. I bow in wonder that God would take two such flawed, rough stones as Jana and me and, through the pressure of cutting and polishing, transform us into sparkling gems with a new measure of value. If someone had told us shortly after Jenny's death that one day we'd be changed and displayed so that others might receive hope from our ordeal, we wouldn't have thought it possible. How could God bring anything beautiful out of such anguish and brokenness?

If you are currently experiencing darkness of the soul, it's likely that you can't conceive of such a thing yourself. Yet isn't it just like God, the One who brings beauty from ashes, to transform us from devastation to glory?

TRANSFORMATION PRODUCES PRAISE

Journey with us back in time, before the Civil War, before Columbus discovered America... back two thousand years to the time of Christ.

It's a cold, dark night. Aromatic fragrances filter through the canopy of silent olive trees. Lying on the ground beneath the canopy is a stone, the One called the Cornerstone.

Listen. You can hear His scream.

Nooooooooo! "My Father... My Father! I beg You, take this cup from me."

The scream is born from what God is asking His Son to do—to pay for the sins of a wicked world with the price of His own innocent blood. Yet woven through the scream is the cry of surrender.

"Not what I want, my Father, but what You want."[4]

Only a few days earlier, Jesus had climbed the mount to Jerusalem, as many of His faithful followers gathered along the road and cried out praises to Him.

"Hosanna! Praise God on high."

The crowds surrounded him, laying palm branches on the ground before Him as an act of worship. But certain men, consumed by jealousy, tried to silence the praise of the crowds with scornful criticism.

"Teacher," they ordered Jesus, "rebuke Your disciples."

Jesus responded, "I tell you, if these become silent, *the stones* will cry out" (Luke 19:38-40, emphasis ours).

Today the faithful roadside disciples have long since departed, their voices silenced. But you and I, His living stones, still cry out.

We, His children, are all screaming stones.

We scream in anguish: "Lord, noooooooooo! Take this cup from me."

We scream in anger: "Lord, why is this happening to me?"

We scream in surrender: "I give up, Lord—not my will, but Yours."

The nature of our scream changes, but ultimately *we will* all *cry out in praise to Him* as polished stones who understand His power and His love.

From anguish to glory, the cycle continues.

This evening, somewhere in the world, a clock ticks quietly in thick apprehension. Suddenly...

Brrrring!

Nooooooooo! The scream of anguish, as another stone is pressed against a spinning lap where its blemishes are polished away.

But then, another scream—an echo *from the future*. Listen. Do you hear it?

"Hosanna!" It's a cry of adoration, as the living stone marvels over the transforming power of God in his life. His cry ascends heavenward and joins the angelic host who proclaim, "Holy, holy, holy is the LORD Almighty! The whole earth is filled with His glory" (Isaiah 6:3, NLT).

2 GEMS

PRAYER:

Lord, thank You for the screams in my life. Thank You for meeting me in my pain. Take my screams and turn them into cries of praise for You.

As a living stone, I scream at God in pain; eventually, God changes my pain to praise.

In the first hours of a crisis:

- Take time to pray—for wisdom, strength, and protection.

- Expect God's enemy, Satan, to attack your mind through accusations of doubt, self-condemnation, or failure. Reject his lies and embrace the truth that God will help you through this trial.

- Seek counsel from a trusted acquaintance who has experienced a similar trial.

- Despair can lead to emotional darkness. Turn on the lights, physical lights around you as well as the spiritual light within you, as you read God's Word aloud (John 1:1-5; 9-13; Colossians 1:9-22; Psalm 23).

CHAPTER

Battered in the Streambed

WHAT A HORRIBLE *way for a seven-year-old boy to spend his day—stuck in this museum looking at "old stuff" with grownups and my pesky sister. Nobody even asked if I cared to come along; they* made *me. I'm sooooo bored.*

What's that up ahead? Hmmm, a dark room and a policeman. What's he guarding? Is that a six-shooter on his belt? Neat!

It was 1962, and I (Jim) meandered through the Witte Museum in San Antonio, Texas, with a chance to acquire some "Texas culture." The only problem was that culture had never been a high priority on this second grader's agenda, and this day trip with parents and relatives already seemed three weeks old.

A welcome diversion appeared ahead. The mysterious room and security guard promised a break from the monotonous glass cases filled with meaningless exhibits.

I eyeballed the guard as we entered the darkness. There, in the middle of the room, stood a glass box on top of a stand.

Why is that small light shining inside the box? There must be something really cool up there.

We approached the pedestal. I stretched on tiptoe to view its mysterious contents. *Ugh, too short.* My dad lifted me to see inside the secured glass case. There, dimly lit and displayed on black velvet, sat

23

the McFarlin Canary Diamond. The nearly flawless, intense-yellow, fifty carat stone beamed like car headlights in this boy's eyes. Brilliant flashes sparkled in spectacular contrast with the black velvet background.

A million questions raced through my mind: *Do all rocks have light inside them or just diamonds? How did that light get in there? How do you make a rock sparkle like that? Why is this room so dark; couldn't we see the diamond better with the lights on?*

The McFarlin exhibit ignited within me a zeal for mineralogy. The earth sciences allured me throughout grade school and into college. Two geology degrees eventually came, then a Ph.D. in geochemistry, followed by a research position in a major mineral company that focused on gold, platinum, and diamond exploration. During the last fifteen years I've cut and polished gemstones as a hobby (for Jana's gemstone obsession!) and for a small business.

The answers to my boyhood questions eventually came with a college education. I learned that not all that sparkles is a diamond; in fact, several minerals possess gem qualities. The mysterious, mesmerizing light that beams from inside a stone actually enters from the outside. The mineral must be transformed by cutting away the flawed portions to form tiny mirrors—facets that allow light to pass inside through its surface and then reflect back out. Each facet must be highly polished. Only a polished gem reflects light into darkness; darkness, in fact, provides the perfect backdrop to view the brilliance of a gem.

The McFarlin exhibit illuminated more than the dark display room; it enlightened the course of my life. When I consider that encounter, the awe that flooded over me and the intense passion birthed within me to find and cut gemstones, I realize that something more was going on than just the simple admiration of a sparkling, yellow stone. Something spiritual stirred my young soul. For years the image lurked deep inside me, though I couldn't put my finger on

The 49.40 carat McFarlin Canary Diamond originally belonged to the Maharajah of Mahratta in the Gujarat region of India.[1] The nearly flawless, canary-yellow, emerald-cut stone was sold for U.S. currency, through a series of transactions, and arrived in New York. E.B. McFarlin, of San Antonio, Texas, eventually purchased the stone in 1956. The McFarlin family presented it to the Witte Museum in San Antonio in 1961, where it was prominently displayed for public view.

On June 4, 1968, a man entered the museum with a lawn chair and a concealed hammer. A gate which descended upon alarm had replaced the security guard who formerly stood at the entrance of the diamond display room. The man left the chair in the doorway of the display room, smashed the glass case with the hammer, removed the diamond, and made his getaway underneath the gate—now blocked by the lawn chair. He was dubbed "The Lawn Chair Bandit."

One year later, a thief captured in Kingsville, Texas, on a different charge confessed to stealing the stone. He reportedly sold it to someone in Phoenix and received only $6,000 for the stone, which was valued at over $365,000. The McFarlin diamond has never been recovered.

it until later in life. Now I understand that this early image revealed to me the contrasting forces of darkness and light. At the end of the chapter, we'll talk more about this, but first let's consider the birth of a natural gemstone and its arduous journey to the display case. It's an amazing process that parallels the spiritual journey of mankind.

THE JOURNEY OF A GEM— FROM BEAUTY TO BLEMISH

"Eeeeyouch! This water's freezin' cold," Jana fussed, shaking her fingers.

"Yep, my hands are stiff, and we've only been at it thirty minutes," I replied. "Can you imagine how tough the old miners must have been to endure this day after day?"

A few minutes passed. "Have you found *anything* that resembles gold?" I asked, with thinning patience.

"Nope. I don't think there ever was gold in this creek. Next time we try this gold panning thing we'll have to bring warm gloves," Jana insisted, while we loaded our gold pans and empty specimen bottles into the backpack.

As we packed the car, she continued. "Did you notice that all the rocks were smooth and round? I thought they'd be jagged or freshly broken but it looks like someone shaped each one."

"Good eye," I replied with a smile. "They've been battered and worn smooth by the turbulent water in the streambed." *How does she do it? Jana's artistic attention to details amazes me! I'm the geologist and even I failed to notice the obvious effects of streambed abrasion.*

The cobbles along this particular streambed were rounded; their dried exteriors were dulled and blemished. Centuries of battering one another in the turbulent water had fractured, abraded, and long altered their original appearance. Gemstones suffer the same fate.

Life in the streambed is rough!

SEPARATION FROM THE MATRIX

Do you know where gemstones are found?

Gravel streambeds and ancient gravel deposits source many of the stones that we cut and polish today. Sapphires, diamonds, and spinels accumulate in a stream with time, similar to gold, by their relative weight and tough durability. They are mined with painstaking labor—hours of washing and sieving buckets of gravel.

The rough stones found in a streambed appear as dull and frosted glassy nodules, but they didn't start that way. Most gemstones began as beautiful crystals birthed within a hard, rock matrix through extreme temperature and pressure. The tough rock matrix protects each delicate crystal from the external forces of nature. Eventually, tiny fractures form and provide conduits in the rock for erosion, chemical weathering, and other corrosive forces. These eventually loosen and free the precious stone. Once free from the matrix, it can never return to the protective safety of the rock on its own accord.

Years of rainfall and transport deposit the crystal into a turbulent streambed. Countless collisions with other stones in the swift, merciless current abrade its surface and reshape the stone into a rough nodule awaiting discovery.

The stone's surface, now blemished and soiled, shields the light that once illuminated its interior. Transparency and beautiful coloration now lie secluded in darkness. Fractures may penetrate its very core. At best, a feeble glow is the only remnant of the crystal's former glory.

The journey of a gemstone provides a startling analogy to the creation and fall of mankind. Both mankind and gemstones were created in beautiful perfection: Both fell from the protection of their rock fortress, and both lay battered and corrupted in the streambed. We've examined the journey of a gemstone from a beautiful crystal to a rough and darkened nodule. Now let's consider mankind's odyssey.

THE FALL OF MAN—
FROM PERFECTION TO PERVERSION

One verse in Genesis reveals God's grand design for mankind from the very beginning:

> God created man *in His own image*, in the *image of God* He created him; male and female he created them.
>
> (Gen. 1:27, emphasis ours)

Man and woman formed the pinnacle of God's creation—His triumphant grand finale of beautiful, richly colored "living stones" that graced His spectacular creation. No other creature enjoyed the privilege of being created "in His image." No imperfections marred His two masterpieces. Light formed the substance of the man and woman's souls.

The husband and wife lived in untainted relationship with their Creator. They enjoyed evening walks and conversations with God, all their needs fully provided. The protective rock matrix of God's love enveloped Adam and Eve, as they dwelled with Him in the Garden. The Divine relationship saturated their souls, as they focused on Him.

Then everything changed.

External forces entered the scene.

You likely know the story.[1] God gave Adam and Eve all things except one—they were forbidden to eat the fruit from the Tree of Knowledge. Satan (the serpent) deceived Eve with a lie: "Eat of the fruit that God has forbidden and you will become like God." Eve's eyes focused on self rather than God. She consumed the fruit, as did Adam who was beside her. In a split second their disobedience became the first sin. Sin blotted out their light from God like a black cloud. And, like a mighty earthquake, sin shattered their foundation and formed a gaping fissure between themselves and God. This is commonly known in theological circles as "the fall of man." It plunged their souls and every future soul into an individual, self-ordained captivity by darkness, separate from the light of God. C.S. Lewis likened the fall to the creation of a new species never intended by God:

> What man lost by the Fall was his original specific nature...Hence, pride and ambition, the desire to be lovely in its own eyes and to depress and humiliate all rivals, envy, and restless search for more, and still more security, were now the attitudes that...came easiest to it...it was the emergence of a new kind of man—a new species never made by God, had sinned itself into existence.[2]

Sin-plagued humans could no longer exist within the blazing light of a pure and holy God.[3] Separation became imperative until God could provide a solution to the issue of sin, so God drove man from the Garden. Immediately, the torrential forces of a hostile world attacked. A flood of miseries swept the crystals out of the garden and deposited them into the hard, challenging world which we label "the streambed of life." Separated from God's Divine protection by a compulsive and destructive sin nature, corruption reigned. Darkness and perversion followed.

DARKNESS IN THE STREAMBED

Marred and fractured gemstones are darkened to physical light.

Marred and fractured living stones are darkened to spiritual light.

After his fall, mankind encountered spiritual darkness. Scripture often speaks of light as the spiritual analogy for righteousness and life. What about darkness? Although not a particularly pleasant topic, let's consider for a moment the scriptural attributes of spiritual darkness. Christian authors often describe darkness simply as the absence of light—in other words, a life lived without Christ.

Is that all there is to it?

If so, why do the multitudes, when presented with the Gospel, not only reject the Good News of Christ but angrily denounce the Word and often persecute the evangelist? Surely something deeper is at work.

Andrew Murray provides an insightful but chilling perspective on spiritual darkness. He points out that it's not only the *absence* of Christ, but the *presence* of an organized host of cruel, demonic beings driven by Satan himself to destroy God's precious stones:

> The world is made up of sinful humanity, not a mere collection of individuals who are led on in their sin by blind chance. It is an organized force that is unknowingly animated by one evil power that fills it with its spirit; it is a power of darkness, led on by one leader, the *"god of this world"* (2 Corinthians 4:4). *"You once walked according to the course of this world, according to the prince of the power of the air, the spirit who now works in the sons of disobedience"* (Ephesians 2:2). [4]

These insights change the playing field. The streamed of life is not a simple babbling brook that we casually wade into with bare feet and rolled-up jeans in order to splash, frolic, and pass the time on a hot afternoon. Rather, it's the perpetual bondage of a blinded race that is so consumed with self that even their own miseries, bondages, and emotional wounds go unnoticed. Murray later adds, "The great power of the world lies in its darkness. The Scriptures tell us, '*The god of this world hath blinded the minds of them which believe not*'" (2 Cor. 4:4).

"*hath blinded the minds...*"

Profound.

This idea makes darkness a bit more evil than merely what "the absence of light" might suggest, doesn't it? Not that Jesus' absence wouldn't be devastating. And yet, mankind doesn't flee the streambed and leave behind its pain and evil. In fact, he seems attached to it. Let's see why.

DECEPTION—THE POWER OF DARKNESS

Painful times come to every man and woman. Some recover and grow stronger through each trial. Others become embittered and self-centered. Why do so many in this world live their lives in the pain of emotional bondage? It's because the cruelty of the streambed enslaves every soul, and Satan's deceptive nature amplifies its allure. Paul described this quality of "the evil one" in 2 Corinthians 11:14-15:

> ...for even Satan disguises himself as an angel of Light...his servants also disguise themselves as servants of righteousness...

Every person without Christ stands helpless against the power of Satan. It reminds me (Jim) of a classic quote from one of my favorite television shows, the Looney Tunes cartoon series. In a rendition of the 1776 American Revolution, the powerful British warrior Yosemite Sam boastfully announced to Bugs Bunny, the weakly armed colonist, "I'm Yosemite Sam, and I've got you outnumbered one-to-one!"

Without Jesus we are each hopelessly outnumbered by Satan.

Scripture clearly states that Satan is a thief and that his desire is to "steal and kill and destroy" God's people (John 10:10). He masterfully weaves our self-centered tendencies into a deadly noose that strangles the life out of mankind. Some theologians regard the perversion of mankind as so dark and so extreme that he is helpless to respond to, or even desire, Christ. It's the perfect endpoint of a "blinded mind." Consider the following comments by R.C. Sproul:

> What is meant by the concept of total depravity is not that man is wicked as he could possibly be. Bad as we are, we can still conceive of ourselves doing worse things than we do. Rather, it means that sin has such a hold upon us in our natural state, that we never have a positive desire for Christ. [5]

Satan *will* accomplish his goals in those outside of Christ and even disguise himself with light if necessary. How often have you heard someone say, "I'm basically a good person"? Such telltale confessions are sulfurous pen strokes that inscribe the deceptive signature of Satan himself. In reality, without Jesus we cycle deeper and deeper into sin's devastating emotional chaos typified by fear, hatred, lust, anger, and self-reliance.

We've experienced several blows of our own in the brutal streambed. Looking back, it seems that certain trauma came simply through life in a sin-infested world. Other situations, in our way of thinking, were orchestrated by Satan specifically to steal, kill, or destroy us. The turbulent waters shaped our attitudes, beliefs and perspectives. We'll share a few of our tumbles in the following sections.

JANA'S TURBULENT WATERS

Stop it! Stop it! I screamed, yet no sound came out.

My tiny five-year-old arms wrapped protectively around Mike, my older stepbrother, whose crumpled body shook with sobs. Trembling with fear, we pressed tightly against the wall and next to the console TV, as we watched the violent scene unfold before us.

My mother punched his mother in the face with her fist. She hit her again…and again…and again.

Crash! They both fell to the floor.

Like a wild animal coming in for a kill, Mother pounced on top of Mike's mother's back. Mother grabbed her hair and smashed her face into our living room floor over and over.

Stop it! Stop it! I tried to scream, but fear welded my throat shut. I stood motionless, petrified that if I made a sound Mother's wrath would turn on me. The electrical heat from the TV next to me burned my bare arm. The pain reminded me that this was no dream; it was real. I squeezed my eyes shut so I would not see the blood. *Why had Mike and I come inside the house to watch cartoons? If only we'd stayed outside and waited for his mother to pick him up maybe this wouldn't have happened. Oh, it's all my fault.*

I don't remember what happened after the fight. I don't remember who broke it up. I don't know where Mike went. I only learned later, as an adult, that Mike's mom suffered stitches and a broken nose and that this event was a climax in a series of episodes which resulted in Mother being committed to a psychiatric institution due to a psychotic episode.

My next memory was that of staring into the blue eyes of a white-haired lady who asked me a question.

"Where ya headed, little ones?" The elderly woman sat down behind me and my eight-year-old brother Hal.

"Our grandparents' house," I sighed, as I leaned against the metal wall next to my seat on the Greyhound bus.

"Ah! A little vacation. How sweet," she chimed.

Hal clinched his teeth and grunted, "Some vacation."

I reached down and rubbed my arm. The heat from the metal side of the bus burned the same place as the television, reminding me of Mother's rage. A million questions raced through my mind. *Why are we being sent away? What did I do to be sent away? Who was that lady who put us on the bus? How long before we get there? Where did those policemen take Mother? Why isn't she coming with us?*

I voiced my questions to Hal. "I don't know. Shut up and don't cry!" Hal folded his arms, closed his eyes, and went to sleep.

Six hours later we arrived safely at my grandparents' house. We had been sent away so quickly that all we had were the clothes on our backs. We stayed with my mother's parents for three months. It was a lonely and confusing time. No one would answer my questions. No one would talk to me. Larry, my stuffed lion, would have talked to me. He had a string in his back that, when you pulled it, made him say the funniest things. But he wasn't here; he was at home in my bedroom. If only I could go home.

If I had known what awaited me, between the years of five and sixteen, maybe I would have been less anxious to return. Mother was diagnosed with Borderline Personality Disorder (BPD). I never knew who would walk in the door wearing her skin—the drama queen, the witch, the waif, or the hermit. Stepfathers came and went like a revolving door... it became a way of life to instantly have a larger family. Some of my stepfathers had children of their own, which meant a shuffle of bedrooms or a move. My older half-brother and I made a list of the number of "husbands" Mother had during her lifetime. I know it seems impossible—I can hardly believe it myself—but recently I found a copy of my third grade report card in which mother had, over the course of the year, signed off with six different names representing the six men she'd married that year. Mother was addicted to men the way an addict is addicted to cocaine.

Obsessed with her figure and looks, Mother always tried to appear sensual. She attempted to teach me to walk, talk, dress, and act sexy so, in her words, "I would always have the upper hand over men." Her constant life lesson was, "You can't live with a man and can't live without one, so use them and lose them."

The bathroom was Mother's meeting room for our "family talks." Hal and I would sit on the side of the tub while she'd tell us the last "daddy" wasn't good enough, and he would never be back or that she had just married the perfect man to be our new daddy. She demanded that I call him "Daddy," or she'd spank me so hard that "I wouldn't be able to sit down for a week."

I didn't want any of these daddies. I only wanted my real dad, who was, sadly, an angry alcoholic who left me when I was six months old. He floated in and out of Hal's and my lives. I hungered for his attention and approval. My heart leapt for joy when he occasionally picked us up for a weekend visit. However, he didn't know what to do with a girl, so he usually dropped me off at a girlfriend's house and spent the time with my brother. He'd tell Mother. "I'll take Hal. You keep 'the girl.'"

As a teenager I could not shed what I'd come to believe as a child, that I had to live up to the expectations of others in order to receive love. Mother expected me to be the perfect daughter, one she could "show off" or brag about. I not only had to have good grades but participate in specific extra-curricular activities, ones she thought were better than others, which increased the tension between us. Mother had married at age fifteen, which prevented her from being active in such events. Now she seemed to want to live her life through me. She insisted that I belong to more social groups such as Future Homemakers of America (FHA, president for two years), the drama club, and the Student Council. But I rebelled by being active in organizations which were more service oriented, such as Teens Aid the Retarded (TARS, president for three years), Girl Scouts (leader), and the Lions Club. At church I was a Bible class teacher, a bus and puppet ministry worker, and an active member in our church youth group. Mother would not give me permission to do what I wanted unless I participated in what she wanted, so I did both. The best part of these activities meant that I was rarely home.

After my freshman year of high school, Hal left for college and I became Mother's daily frustration scapegoat. Life with her became unbearable. That summer I decided to move to Houston and live with my father and try to earn his favor. I thought if I took care of my five-year-old half-brother, who now lived with my dad, he'd be forced to like me. Sure, I'd miss my friends, but at least I wouldn't have to deal with Mother's unpredictable nature. I tried to think positively about being "unpaid help" for my father. *I won't mind taking care of my little brother, cooking, cleaning, and doing laundry. I'll be the lady of the house, and the special treatment will be fun.*

Instantly "Little John" and I bonded. I cared for him while my father went to work and even on the weekends.

Then came the promise of a fun trip—a vacation to inaugurate my father's new motorhome. I folded Little John's blue shirt and placed it in the suitcase next to my own shorts and pants. *Gotta get everything packed. One more trip to the laundromat and I think that's it.*

I'm not sure what I heard first, the slamming door or the slurred stream of vulgar names my father spewed, as he searched the apartment for me.

I hated it when he came home drunk.

"I'm in here putting Little John's clothes away," I responded to his call with forced cheerfulness.

"Come give your daddy a big hug and kisses," he said, as he entered the room and tripped on a toy.

Little John quickly bolted to hide behind the door.

I wasn't as lucky.

I ripped free of his arms and groping hands, grabbed Little John, and ran down the apartment stairs. We fled to the laundromat. Out of the corner of my eye, I saw him stumble down the stairs. In a movie, I'd seen how to prop a chair against a door to keep people from entering.

It worked.

I scooped Little John up into my lap, felt the laundry money in my pocket, and spied the payphone.

"It's going to be okay." I whispered in my little brother's ear, as I pulled out a coin to place a call for help.

As I think back on my childhood streambed, I'd rate my life in the streambed as Class 5 whitewater rapids marked by sharp drops and twisting turbulence. I'll let Jim tell you about his life in the streambed as a young boy.

JIM'S ABRASIVE CURRENTS

"This is a radish. This is an onion. These are tomato plants."

I was in heaven.

Summer days normally crawled by for this five-year-old boy, but this late afternoon zipped by in a blur. My dad and I were spending time together in his garden. He was particularly proud of his tomatoes.

"Why are you pulling up *those* plants?" I asked, with endless curiosity.

"They're weeds. They use the good plants' water," he explained. "I pull them up so they won't take over the garden."

I didn't fully understand but I yearned to help. I always wanted to help him. He was my TV Western hero—my John Wayne and Paladin—and I yearned to be just like him. My enthusiasm kicked in and I reached down and pulled up a "weed"—an "onion weed."

"WHAT ARE YOU DOING?!" my dad's voice echoed.

Instantly I dropped the young plant; my shoulders slumped, and I dreaded what might follow.

"I was just help'n you pull up the weeds."

"That's an onion. I just showed it to you. Now get out of the garden, and don't pull up any more plants!"

My hero vanished. In his place stood the man that I feared above all else, the angry dad. Although I yearned to be with Dad, close to him, his short temper and eruptive anger kept me constantly wary. I retreated from the vegetable plot immeasurably relieved nothing worse had happened.

The next day, Kathy, my "girlfriend" from next door, came over. We often spent the long afternoons playing together in our backyards. Looking back, I chuckle at the great chivalry I affectionately lavished upon her; it must be genetic in young boys. I protected her from endless bands of imaginary Indians, married her countless times, and even swatted down a wasp nest with a dinner spoon (only once) to demonstrate my valor. This particular afternoon I couldn't wait to impress her with my new knowledge of vegetables.

"That's an ong-yun, and that's a radiss, and back there—those are weeds."

I thoughtlessly stepped into the garden and strained to pull up a very large weed—a "tomato weed."

With perfect timing my mother shouted through the screened back door, "Are you in your dad's garden? What are you doing in there? I'm gonna tell him when he gets home!"

That was the second-most dreaded thing in my young life—the wait for my dad's return from work, knowing Mom would inform him of my disobedience. My valor failed, and I had no enthusiasm for further play. Kathy went home.

Each minute of the remaining afternoon flowed like cold, stiff molasses. I waited, with no concept of time and strained to hear each car that passed on the street.

A slowing car... the car door... he's here....

Another eternity passed... and then the screen door swung open. My dad stepped outside.

Oh no! He's really angry.

The scowl on his face instantly revealed a fierce anger that terrified me.

With giant steps that devoured the ground between us, he grabbed my upper arm and jerked me over to the garden plot. I can't remember much of what happened next or the words he spoke. I do remember how he picked up the large tomato plant I had pulled up earlier that afternoon and lashed my bare legs with the rough, coarse plant and the ball of roots and dirt. My punishment seemed to last forever.

At bath time Mom cleansed my dirty and welted legs.

Compared to Jana's volatile childhood, my early years were a piece of cake. Yet, even though I enjoyed a more stable home environment, sin's destructive presence flowed through our family streambed.

Daddy's anger was likely the result of his own childhood traumas. Brief accounts from his early days revealed a depression-era farming family stressed through hard work with a budget that bordered on poverty. Severe lashings were common from his dad as well. I say this not to excuse his anger but rather to explain it. I had to find ways to deal with his perplexing and unpredictable mood swings that cycled between an active, too-busy lifestyle and a sullen, silent anger that forced me to tiptoe around in self-preservation. Later in my teen years, we seemed closest when working together on the family ranch. I yearned to please him and labored my hardest to gain his approval, which erroneously taught me that love is something that must be earned, rather than a gift freely given.

One other childhood experience deserves mention. I occasionally played in the backyard of another friend. His dad was into pornography. My friend and I—tender four- and five-year-old boys—often snuck out to his parents' storage shed and viewed the magazines' erotic pictures. Those images snared my young soul in a steel-jawed trap of bondage, creating strong, dark currents that pulled me in directions later in life that I struggled to resist. I'll discuss this more in later chapters.

What events have shaped you? The death of someone you love? An unstable childhood? A painful divorce? Dabbling in the occult? What has ground you down and battered you to the point that it's changed the very shape of who you are?

We've said it before, but it bears repeating: Because of our fallen world, a dark and hostile streambed greets every man and woman at birth. Early childhood wounds flaw our character and darken our vision of God. Satan intensifies the darkness by adding deceptions that twist our perceptions of ourselves and our circumstances. We react by applying false emotional bandages of denial, isolation and anger to cover our wounds. More crises come: Illness, traumatic loss, and victimization drive us even further into the suffocating blackness of demonic perversion. We cope by applying additional bandages. We learn to protect "self" at all costs, rather than seeking God and trusting His healing power. Ironically, Satan obliges our self-protective efforts by blinding our view of God, His love and His light.

The streambed aims to grind us to dust.

But wait; there is hope.

God sees our dilemma.

He has not forgotten.

HOPE IN THE STREAMBED

Flawed and blemished nodules are helpless to escape the turbulent waters of life. They simply roll along, coping with the pain and misery of life's dark delusions. Occasionally, though, a glimmer stirs the soul. It comes in unexpected moments that arouse sensations of eternality: the soft cry of a newborn infant; the image of a beautiful galaxy across deep space, as snapped by the Hubble telescope; the unmistakable display of genuine love, as a groom slips a ring on the finger of his bride.

In these moments we *know* there is more to life than the daily stress and collisions of the streambed—something ineffable, something inconceivable, something unimaginably larger than ourselves. We sense peace and the security of refuge within a massive, towering Rock; and we sense a distant former glory of ourselves as we were meant to be. The scenes tug at our soul, as if attempting to lift us from the very streambed itself.

This "something" is, in reality, a Someone.

Jesus.

Hope arises because this One, this Son of God, is not far off. We need not travel through galaxies or time zones to find Him. He is as near as the cry of our heart. Jesus is with us...here in the turbulent waters...here in the streambed. He sees each wounding blow that mars us. He aches with our distress.

Jesus doesn't force us to love Him; He waits for us to choose. At some point we *will* make a choice between Jesus or the streambed. If we choose Jesus we are changed. We lose our dull countenance and begin to glow with the light of His love.

Can we take a moment and shift the focus upon you? How are you doing? Are you being incessantly pounded by cruel blows in the streambed? And yet, do you sense a greater destiny...a strange glow...something much grander than what you've experienced in the turbulent water? The darkness of the streambed doesn't *have* to reign; in fact, it *can't* reign in the light of God's presence.

You are a living stone.

God, the Master Lapidary, is calling you. He desires to reveal the light you were created to display. If you are willing, He will cut and shape, polish and perfect you, until His light shines forth with the brilliance of the McFarlin diamond. Are you ready? Turn the page. You'll discover how God plans to display His glory within you, and we are confident of this: If you open your heart and mind, what you learn will change your life.

J² GEMS

PRAYER:

Dear God, I now recognize that Satan and the painful situations in my past have shaped me in harmful ways. First, I pray for protection from the devil, who darkens and limits my vision of You. Second, I ask that You reveal the personal wounds that have shaped me. And as You do, I trust You will perform a healing work within me, and let Your light reveal the precious living stone I was meant to be.

Battering from the streambed of life creates fractures in my soul.

In the chaos of the streambed:

- Continue to seek and press into God.
- Realize that the enemy will attack you, but God is able to rescue you.
- Ask God to comfort you and heal your most painful wound—then watch carefully to see the results, and record them.

Glimmer in the Gravel

I (JIM) WAS FOUR years old when I found my first diamond.

The locals called the barren strip of land that bordered our Texas home an "unpaved alley." To my young eyes it was foreign territory that promised exotic discoveries. This unexplored land surely held tantalizing deposits of gold, silver, and precious stones, and I resolved to leave no cobble unturned.

On that sunny, summer morning, irresistible temptations lured me beyond the hedgerows and into the alley. Just ahead crept my loyal scout and prospector companion, Frisky, our tabby cat. Behind me squeaked the wheels of the rugged ore cart, a Western Flyer® red wagon, which would haul our treasures home.

I carefully scanned the pebbled landscape.

A glimmer caught my eye in the rocky soil.

There! A flash inside that rock!

Excitement churned, as I picked up the piece of ordinary red sandstone. Tiny mica flakes sparkled in the sunshine. I'd seen the same sparkle in my mom's wedding ring.

Diamonds!

Quickly, I gathered the loose cobbles and kicked up others with the toe of my Keds® tennis shoe. Frisky searched the area for other subtle gleams.

Must keep 'em safe, but where? I know. Back home, in the front yard. Carefully I loaded the valuable specimens and Frisky into the cart and hauled the precious load home. I stashed our treasure next to the porch and raced into the house.

"Mom, come look. I found diamonds!" She stepped out on the front porch and surveyed my valuable ore. Although intrigued, her level of excitement clearly lagged behind my own. Even Frisky wandered off, shaken and disinterested after the rough ride home.

I'll show 'em. I'll find bigger diamonds. I returned to the mine site with rake and shovel. Only much persuasion by a patient mom convinced me to dump the next load near the alley rather than on the front steps, where I'd chosen to "display" my precious gems.

My valiant efforts unearthed not a single precious stone from the alley diamond mine, but I gained a rich education. Bruised toes and smashed fingers taught me about the perils of mining. Another lesson: "All that sparkles is not diamonds" provided a dose of reality. I would eventually learn the value of accurate mineral identification.

Although my treasure proved false, it unveiled within me another deep passion. Just as the McFarlin diamond exhibit (Chapter 2) exposed mysterious cravings to understand and cut gemstones, the alley diamond mine birthed within me powerful yearnings to find and understand the precious stones themselves. I became obsessed with the study of minerals and their crystal forms. Exhilarating gemstone discoveries filled my grade school dreams—large canary diamonds, gemmy amethyst crystals, and rare blue topaz. When I was in fourth grade, my parents gave me a college-level mineralogy book. Mesmerized, I studied the pictures of mineral specimens for hours. I scoured the creeks and fields surrounding our country home day after day searching for a glimmer of a crystal. Discoveries came—an occasional arrowhead or chunk of petrified wood—but no stones of gem quality.

Time slipped by. I matured, and so did my passion for geology. At age sixteen a driver's license opened new frontiers for mineral exploration. Freedom at last—gemstones in sight! The nearest occurrence of natural rough lay two hours west of Austin. Ranchers had picked up nodules of an unusual blue, gem-quality topaz in the granite hills since the early 1900s. Surely other gems lay hidden in those hills. I studied maps and packed shovels, trowels, and rakes in anticipation of my gemstone hunting expedition. Finally, the day came. I cajoled a buddy to accompany me, and we raced down the highway to imminent discoveries.

Just pay the rancher a small fee and search his land for the elusive Texas blue topaz. For most of one day, we scoured the hot, dusty, cactus- and mesquite-covered countryside in search of a glimmer of blue light. We raked the surface, dug through parched, crusty soil, and examined hundreds of pieces of ordinary quartz. My buddy complained that scores of other prospectors had sifted this soil, and they'd left behind nothing of value for greenhorns like us. His interest waned, just as Frisky's had many years earlier. With aching backs, dust-caked faces, and parched expectations, we dragged ourselves home empty-handed.

THE THRILL OF DISCOVERY

If a gemstone is a thing of rare value that's filled with inherent light, then six years later I discovered my first precious jewel. Her name was Jana. I asked her to marry me and she said "yes."

As starving Texas A&M newlyweds, we were madly in love, but we also faced personal adjustments, as we learned to live together under one roof. I was surprised when details I thought I understood—who washed the dishes, *how* to wash a dish, and *how* to squeeze a toothpaste tube—were called into question. Jana had her own surprises, one of which came two years into our marriage, while en route to visit potential graduate schools to further my geochemistry education. Suddenly, Jana's young husband slammed on the brakes, leapt out of the car, and raced across the 106-degree, rattlesnake-infested desert in the middle of West Texas. The reason? To gather Balmorhea blue agate, a semi-precious stone.

After grad school, the carefree joys of early marriage morphed into the hard realities of life. We purchased our first house and birthed two children while I thrashed to stay afloat in a demanding research position that required considerable travel. Life got complicated. Jana struggled to raise our daughters while I spent weeks away on business trips. The daily stress of raising a young family and managing a strenuous career dimmed my gemstone cravings into a faint and distant glimmer. But then, a new work project in Butte, Montana, revived my dwindling passion. At first, Butte seemed like any other place—another restaurant, another parking lot, another hotel lobby. But this hotel lobby offered a unique distraction: A brochure advertised "Gemstone Adventures." I decided to visit the nearby canyon that Saturday to help pass the time.

Simply pay the rancher a small fee, and sieve the gravel. Dismissing memories of my unsuccessful search for Texas blue topaz a decade earlier, I drove to the site, paid the fee, and received a bucket of wet sediment freshly dredged from the adjacent stream. A simple wooden frame with tubs of icy stream water stood nearby and served as a work table. I washed and sieved the silty gravel. Clean canyon air fragranced by the resinous needles of nearby spruce filtered through my senses, as sand and clay filtered through the screen. A matrix of BB-sized gray pebbles and coarse cobbles remained in the sieve, awaiting examination.

Then I saw it. A glimmer.

A quarter-inch stone with an unmistakable greenish-blue glow seemed radiant among the smaller pebbles. I picked up the stone. It glowed like wet frosted glass in vivid contrast with the monotonous gray gravel.

"Eureka!" A gem-quality Montana sapphire.

I found others that day in a variety of colors—green, blue, pink, violet. Most were less than a carat in size. A few approached two carats, just large enough to facet. After thirty years my dreams had been realized. Temporary satisfaction flowed through my soul but it didn't quench the thirst; in fact these small discoveries fueled my passion for finding gemstones. A few years later Jana and I purchased a faceting machine and the search for rough continued.

Simply pay the rancher a (more substantial) fee, and sieve the gravel. Twenty-five years after Butte, Jana and I, now empty nesters, found ourselves on a hot, remote hillside in Southern California in quest

---

A richly colored sapphire of high clarity is stunningly precious and second only to diamond in hardness. Their density and hardness cause the natural stones to be concentrated in streambeds where they are mined by sieving and laboriously working the gravel.

Sapphires exhibit a rainbow of colors. The highest quality stones are a vivid, medium-dark blue currently produced in Sri Lanka, Thailand, and Eastern Australia. Commercial production also occurred in the United States. The Yogo mine in western Montana produced beautiful, natural "cornflower" blue stones valued at approximately $2000 per carat (cut gemstone) in 1993. The retail price of a one carat stone from Sri Lanka of similar quality the same year was approximately $500.[1]

of gem-quality tourmaline rough. Green and pink gemmy tourmaline sparkled in the rubble from a famous mine. We gasped as the wet-sieved stones glimmered like frosted shards of pink and green glass against a dark gravel matrix.

What is it about the glimmer that thrills me?

I can't explain the tantalizing allure. Perhaps it's the "Eureka!"—the riveting moment of discovery of a precious stone against a dull matrix of ordinary rock. Or perhaps it's the visual contrast between a glowing stone of incredible value mixed among common gravel. Or maybe it's the intriguing way light illuminates the stone's dull surface and begs for its internal beauty to be revealed. Whatever the reason, my heart exults with the glimpse of a glimmer.

Even now I recall the intense childhood emotions fueled by those deceptive "sparkles" in the ordinary alley sandstone. A curious, perhaps even sacred awe captures my imagination, and my thoughts drift heavenward. I meditate upon a wondrous scene—an analogy contrived only by a mineralogist—and I wonder: Does God see me this way? Does He look down on the dull and blemished streambed of humanity and see me, a living stone, crying out to Him, as a glimmer in the gravel?

ILLUMINATED IN THE STREAMBED

The Lord has looked down from heaven upon the sons of men to see if there are any who understand, who seek after God.
(Psalm 14:2)

Imagine God, as He looks down upon the streambed of humanity. He sees a myriad of stones that have broken away from the matrix of His love through disobedience. He scans the battered stones.

Looking...searching...for a heart that seeks after Him. Suddenly a glimmer catches His eye—a colorful stone with a subtle glow that stands out among the dark matrix. The glimmer excites Him and delights His heart. He spent an eternity waiting for this moment.

Here is one who seeks Him, one who longs to know His Creator. Beneath the stone's blemished surface a receptive heart glows with desire to know, to understand, and to intertwine in true relationship with its Maker. This is the glimmer in the gravel: a heart that cries out for intimacy with his Creator.

"What's so special about a simple glowing stone?" you might ask.

Don't underestimate the value of that subtle glow. Physical battles are fought over deposits of precious gemstone rough. Spiritual battles are also fought over living stones. Fortunately for our sakes, Christ fought and won the spiritual war on the cross for mankind. "He's crazy about us,"[1] and we're precious in His sight.

Let's consider just how passionately God pursues a glowing stone. We'll share the accounts of two such stones from Scripture: Nicodemus, a pious man whose religion failed to satisfy the longings of his soul, and the woman at the well, who discovered that her greatest need was *not* for the love of a man but for the love of God.

A GLIMMER: A RELIGIOUS MAN SEEKS GOD

What was I thinking? Why would I even dare to ask the Great Teacher to meet me, and why would He come at such a late hour? At least the thick darkness hides me from the watchful eyes of my Pharisaical brethren who vehemently disapprove of this man.

Why do they despise Jesus? Has jealousy fully enslaved their hearts? They'd stone me if they learned I requested to meet with the one they call "the devil."[2] *Still, He has great wisdom... He silences the scribes! He must know the answer, and I have to hear it. I must find the real God of Abraham.*

Nicodemus, a respected Pharisee and teacher of the Law, ached with internal conflict. His dogged obedience to fulfill the demands of the Mosaic Law left him with a gnawing sense that religion, in itself, was not soul-satisfying. He wanted more; he sought true relationship with God.

Have I done enough? I tithed this morning on the gift of dill seeds from my neighbor. I prayed two hours. I studied the Scriptures. How can I know God accepts me?

The Almighty seems distant; striving with the Law seems pointless. These endless traditions and laws never burdened our father Abraham, yet the Almighty loved him and even spoke to him. Oh how I yearn for just a single word of confirmation from God that He even knows me.

And this Jesus. Who is He really? The crowds call Him the Great Teacher. Others whisper that He is God's Prophet—the Messiah, yet how could the Prophet come from Capernaum when Scripture speaks of Bethlehem?[3] *And why does my heart burn when I hear of the miracles He performs: The blind see, the lame walk, and even the dead live. No one could do these things unless empowered by God.*

There He is! He did come!

Jesus met Nicodemus that evening under the cover of darkness. In the black of night, our Lord perceived a glimmer—the flickering desire in Nicodemus' soul to know, to really know, God.

Jesus told Nicodemus that if he wanted to enter the Kingdom of God he had to be "born again."

Bewildered, Nicodemus asked, "How can a man be born when he is old? He cannot enter a second time into his mother's womb and be born, can he?"[4]

Jesus explained that two births are required: first, a birth of the flesh, and second, a birth of the spirit. He told Nicodemus that God loved the world and sent His only son (Jesus) to die for all of mankind's sins. He would be lifted up on a cross so that all could look upon Him and witness His sacrificial death.[5] All who believed and accepted His death as payment for their own sin would be born of the Spirit—the second birth. They would receive eternal life and immediately enter into relationship with God Himself.

Could it really be so simple? Could a relationship with God be anchored through this Man? Could He really be God's Son? The Psalms speak of the Son—God's Anointed One.[6] *But now? In my lifetime? Speaking to me?*

Ironically, Jesus ended their discussion under the cover of darkness with a lesson on light. "Light has come into the world," Jesus said. [7]

Nicodemus pondered His words. *Jesus must be talking about Himself... that HE is the light! But what does that mean?*

Jesus continued, "He who practices the truth comes to the light."[8] *Now He must be talking about me. I practice truth as I know it, and I have come to Him, the light.*

We don't know exactly how this encounter with Jesus impacted Nicodemus. The Bible is silent on the details, but we speculate that a visible change occurred in the heart of this Pharisee. The heart of this living stone yearned to know God and glowed with a faint glimmer; the glimmer surely intensified after he encountered God's Son, the light of the world.

A GLIMMER: A SINFUL WOMAN SEEKS GOD

Noontime is no time to visit this well, but it's easier to bear the heat of the sun than the fiery contempt in the faces of my former friends.

This wasn't the life I'd dreamed of; I thought I'd marry one man, grow old with him, birth him a son—many sons. And now Andrew barely speaks to me. He'll take me as his lover but not as his wife. He's no different than all the others. I've known this dark tension five times with five different men. Each used me, and when they'd had their fill, they tossed me aside like a dirty rag.

God, no man has ever valued me, but do You value me? Could I dare hope that I have worth in Your eyes? Please be merciful to me, a sinner. Please help me. I need to know that You see me and care for me.

Who sits at the well in this heat? A Jewish man? No worries, he will flee like the desert mist when he sees me approach. Jews treat us Samaritans like dogs, and this nameless Jew certainly would not value me.

Why does He remain as I draw my water? Why does He look at me? Will He harm me? Oh God, please help me.

"Give Me a drink."

Startled, the woman looked at the stranger. He seemed harmless enough. She asked Him, "How is it that You, being a Jew, ask me for a drink since I am a Samaritan woman?"

The man replied, "If you knew the gift of God, and who it is who says to you, 'Give Me a drink,' you would have asked Him, and He would have given you living water."[9]

Her brow lifted, puzzled. His words created consternation. *What does this man want from me? Whatever it is, it's not what other men desire; such men only take, but this man wants to give me something. Something called "living water"—but what is that?*

"Sir, give me this water so I will not be thirsty, nor come all the way here to draw."

And then an odd exchange: Bring Me your husband...I have no husband...It's true; you've had five other husbands and the man you currently live with is not your husband.[10]

How could it be? He knows details of my past that no one could ever know, distant memories even I have tried to forget. This is no ordinary man. Could He be a prophet from God? God, have You sent this man to answer the questions burning in my heart, questions no one else will bother to discuss with me?

His eyes do not judge. Instead, they invite my questions. Dare I risk it? Dare I go deeper with this man?

"Sir," the woman said as she laid aside her water pot, "I perceive that You are a prophet."

The man smiled, bolstering her courage to probe more deeply. "Where is the right place to worship? We Samaritans believe it is on this mountain, but you Jews worship in Jerusalem."

What He said surprised and astounded her. He told her a time was coming, and in fact that time was now, when Jews and Samaritans would be less concerned about the proper place of worship and more concerned about the attitude of their hearts. If this were not startling enough, this man called God His Father. And He said that His Father was seeking true worshipers, people who would worship in spirit and in truth.[11]

Her mind raced. His words ignited a fire in her heart. It was as if He were inviting her to call God "Father." He was challenging her to become a true worshiper. As she looked into the burning light of His eyes, she saw something reflected in them, something she'd rarely seen—her own value. It was all too much to take in. It took every bit of restraint she could muster to keep from hugging this man and dancing around the well.

Who was this man? Could it be... was it possible... dare she ask the question that burned in her soul?

"I know that Messiah is coming," she said, "and when He comes he will explain everything to us."

The man's eyes twinkled. A smile lifted his bearded cheeks. He leaned forward and whispered the words she would replay in her mind for many years to come: "I who speak to you am He."[12]

JESUS: THE ONE TRUE LIGHT

If you've ever traveled at night, you've undoubtedly crossed a railroad track and seen the distant headlight, miles away, of an approaching train. The beam announces the train's arrival long before it reaches the station. The image also reminds us of Christ's entry into our world.

Jesus entered the world as the One True Light. His light shone visibly for centuries before He arrived through the words of prophesy in the Old Testament. Isaiah referred to Jesus as a "light to the nations" *six hundred years* before His birth:

> The people who walk in darkness will see a great light; those who live in a dark land, the light will shine on them. You shall multiply the nation, You shall increase their gladness....
>
> (Isaiah 9:2-3)

Many years later Zacharias prophesied of Jesus' luminous nature by referencing Isaiah 9:2: "...the Sunrise from on high will visit us, to shine upon those who sit in darkness..." (Luke 1:78, 79).

For centuries mankind groped about in the darkness of the streambed, separated from God by sin. These and other passages emphasize that Jesus and His light would enter the world, pierce our spiritual darkness, and shine upon us. His blazing light flooded the darkness that we discussed in the last chapter—both the universal darkness produced by Satan's reign as the god of this world and a personal darkness that emanated from man's sinful choices.

Just what is the "light of Jesus"?

Some rationalize that it's simply His influence—His presence and power in a sin-darkened world. That's a good start, but Scripture hints at something much more basic—an *essential* element to mankind. Notice how John describes light in his Gospel account:

> In Him was life; and *the life was the light of men.* And the light *shines in the darkness,* and the darkness did not comprehend it...There was the true light which, coming into the world, enlightens *every* man.
>
> (John 1:4, 5, 9, emphasis ours)

Do you see it?

John's verses harbor three profound truths that describe Jesus' light and its powerful influence on mankind. Let's explore these principles and better understand how the spiritual light of Jesus impacts both mankind at large and us as individuals.

The first truth is universal: Jesus' light brings life, and this life is available to all mankind. Jesus is the light of the *world*. He is not the light of one city or a single nation—He is the light that "enlightens *every* man [person]"[13] (emphasis ours).

The light of Jesus is all-inclusive. His spiritual light is available to rich and poor, male and female, black and white, every nationality and language. All are invited to embrace the light of Christ. Sadly, not all choose to do so.

The powerful light of Jesus thrusts the heart into a pivotal dilemma with only two options: We can welcome the illuminating influence of His light and life, or we can flee and hide in the deceptive safety of a dark and sulfurous subterranean world ruled by Satan himself. The first choice leads to the birth of a glowing stone, one who glimmers with the promise of eternal life. The second choice leads to eventual death in the darkness of the streambed.

You are probably familiar with the words in John 3:16: "For God so loved the world that He gave His only begotten Son, that whoever believes in Him shall not perish, but have eternal life." But have you ever considered the connection between the life talked about in this verse and the light of Jesus? Light and life are inextricably woven together. When you believe in the *Light*, you receive His *life*. In the moment of belief, His light and life permeate your soul, and *you* become a light, a small reflection of the One True Light. Jesus said, "I am the light of the world," but then, speaking of His Light in us He says, "*You* are the light of the world"[14] (emphasis ours). He adds, "Let your light shine before men that they may see your good deeds and praise your Father in heaven."[15]

Like Nicodemus and the woman at the well, we must receive His light—that is, we must choose to believe and act upon His words. The next two principles of spiritual light build upon our decision to believe.

The second truth is purposeful: Jesus' light exposes sin. Just as light from a window exposes dust on the shelf, the light of Jesus exposes the dirty residue of sin in our darkened lives. His fierce and penetrating light reveals every dirty smudge, from the blatant faults down to the secret sins that stain our heart. Consider the following Scriptures:

> You have placed our iniquities before You, our secret sins in the light of Your presence.
> (Psalm 90:8)

> For nothing is hidden that will not become evident, nor anything secret that will not be known and come to light.
> (Luke 8:17)

Unfortunately, mankind often prefers darkness—their minds blinded to the light of the Gospel by Satan himself (2 Corinthians 4:4). John's Gospel paints a bleak picture of this dark wasteland:

> This is the judgment, that the light has come into the world, and men loved the darkness rather than the light, for their deeds were evil. For everyone who does evil hates the light, and does not come to the light for fear that his deeds will be exposed.
> (John 3:19, 20)

Natural man lives in rebellion toward God, captivated by his selfish desires and thoughts. In other words, "self" rules with no inclination to submit to another authority, especially to a holy God who demands that sin be exposed and expelled in order to live in the purity of His fellowship.

The one who believes in Jesus welcomes His spotlight on sin and invites Jesus' light to penetrate the rough and calloused surface of a battered soul. Like David we cry:

> Search me, O God, and know my heart; try me and know my anxious thoughts; see if there be any hurtful way in me, and lead me in the everlasting way.
> (Psalm 139:23, 24)

Nicodemus and the woman at the well thirsted for intimate relationship with Jesus. We, too, should yearn to live in His light. It exposes our sinful darkness and promotes intimacy with God. We, then, will abhor our darkness and lay it before the Lord, and rejoice in this truth: "My God turns my darkness into light" (Psalm 18:28).

The third truth is personal: The power of His light transforms each individual who surrenders to it. God, The Master Lapidary, sees our "rough" state. He sees the blemishes, the marred edges, the dark places that must be ground and polished away if we are to become the beautifully crafted gem that He envisions. He yearns to transform each of us, and He knows exactly what steps He must take in order to bring about the design in His mind.

Transformation can happen in a flash, but more often it's a lifelong process, one we'll address at length in the chapters ahead. As God's blazing light penetrates our lives it *will* overpower all darkness that is surrendered to Him; however, the intensity of His brilliance is simply more than we can bear in an instant. That's why he changes us through a process that requires time. Charles Spurgeon put it this way:

> When the light of Divine grace first visits a man, it shines with feeble beam. Man by nature is, like a house shut up, the windows of which are all boarded over. Grace does not open every window at once and bid the sun stream in upon weak eyes accustomed to darkness. It rather takes down a part of a shutter at a time...that one may be able to bear it by degrees. The window of man's soul is so thickly encrusted with dirt, so thoroughly begrimed, that no light at all can penetrate it, till one layer is taken off, and a little yellow light is seen; and then another is removed, and then another, still admitting more light, and clearer.[16]

God's light accomplishes much of our transformation, but we also have a role to play. We must choose to surrender, choose to intentionally focus upon His light, and lastly, choose to avoid darkness. Paul explains it further:

> Therefore do not be partakers with them; *for you were formerly darkness, but now you are Light in the Lord; walk as children of Light*...trying to learn what is pleasing to the Lord. Do not participate in the unfruitful deeds of darkness, but instead even expose them.
> (Ephesians 5:7, 8, emphasis ours)

Even though I (Jim) have been a Christian for many years, I sometimes feel that windows in my soul are still boarded over—that shadows, rather than Sunlight, dwell in the hidden recesses of my heart. I ponder how to expose the deeds of darkness when it seems those deeds still grip me. And then suddenly, perhaps in a moment of prayer or when reading God's Word, light beams break through and expose my doubts, my guilt, or even a bondage of which I was unaware. This is the power of His light living within me. It happens over and over. I've learned that, with every dark corner I surrender to Him, He illuminates another room in my house, and the transformation continues.

Beams pierce the darkness of lingering night,
As daisies and dahlias awake from slumber.
Slowly, each blossom in relentless quest
Turns to face this radiant guest;
And faithfully, through sightless eyes, they track His march across
 the sky,
Enthralled with Light and birthed on high.
—*James Chatham*

THE MUSINGS OF A LAPIDARY
Light.

This single word summarizes the entirety of this chapter. As a young boy I was inexplicably drawn to light that glimmered in the gravel. As a young man, my search for light continued. Even now I recall with clarity that warm, sunny afternoon beside the flowing Montana stream when I first spied the glow of the rough, blue-green sapphire against the dark gray pebbles in my sieve. My heart pounded, as I picked up the rough stone and examined its beauty. I rotated it in my hand, imagining its future design. An image emerged—a beautiful blue-green gem set within a delicate gold pendant: All who gazed upon its brilliant reflections would gasp in awe.

From that moment forward a new destiny had been declared for this stone. No longer would it be battered and marred by the pounding of turbulent waters. I had chosen and set it apart from all other stones in the streambed. Yes, abrasion and pressure would come—the tools of transformation—but I would carefully limit and control these forces, in order to transform this sapphire into the beautiful gemstone it was destined to become. It had no concept of its true value. Indeed, its worth would only be realized with surrender to my plans.

In the remainder of this book, we'll take you step by step through the physical transformation of our rough, uncut ametrine into a brilliant gem. With each step, Jana and I will propose similar steps of spiritual transformation that God, the Master Lapidary, applies to us, His living stones. The release of light is the common goal.

Keep in mind, however, that one significant difference can thwart the process: The ametrine *must* submit to my design; it has no choice. You, as a living stone, have a choice. God gave you free will. You can choose to submit to His plans to release His light within you, or you can refuse His plan and succumb to the darkness that will eventually overtake your soul.

What will you choose? Will you allow the light and life of Jesus to flood your heart and mind? Will you submit to His holy light so He can expose and break the power of sin in your life? Will you allow Him to transform you and release His light within you one facet at a time? If so, we invite you to pray this prayer of surrender and ask the Master Lapidary to release the transforming power of His light into your life.

2 GEMS

PRAYER:

God, I have not followed You with my whole heart. I've tried to live life on my own. Forgive me. I surrender and give You permission to shape me according to Your specific design. Search my heart. Extinguish all darkness by the power of Your holy light. Help me to know that, despite my flaws, despite my brokenness, You will change me and use me for Your glory. I commit myself from this moment forward to follow Your Son Jesus and to walk in the light of His power.

When I accept Jesus as Savior, His light illuminates me, and I become a glimmer in the gravel. Jesus is the light of the world.

- Ask Jesus to enlighten the dark streambed around you and make you aware of any deception.

- Ask Jesus to illuminate any "dark rooms" in your soul. Thank Him that He turns darkness into light.

- Pray that He enlightens your friends, neighbors, and relatives who are still living in darkness.

CHAPTER 4

Birthmarks and Blemishes

IMAGINE GOD, THE Master Lapidary, as He sits upon His heavenly throne. Brilliant light floods even the most secluded corner of His throne room, vanquishing darkness. Angelic voices sing ethereal choruses of harmonious praise. Clouds of prayers arise like plumes of sweet incense and envelope the heavenly host.

In His hand the Master Lapidary holds a precious living stone. You.

God peers beneath your blemished surface and delights in the weak but precious glow—the telltale sign of a heart that desires to know Him. His considers your future—the majestic plans and unimaginable wonders prepared specifically for you.[1] Even in your current "rough" state God sees the *future* you, a dazzling gem strategically positioned to display His splendor.

He turns you in His hand and considers the many possibilities: How will you best release the light of Christ so that the fullness of His glory is displayed?

Damaged areas must be cut away. Flaws must be removed. These prevent His light from shining forth. He peers deep into your soul and traces the birthmarks and blemishes acquired in the chaotic, sin-filled world in which you live: fractures of distrust that resulted from wounding lies; threads of insecurity from past incidents where you were overlooked and forgotten; clouds of fear and sorrow that darken your heart because of devastating losses you experienced.

A pattern forms in His mind as He contemplates the perfect design. Cutting and polishing will follow. He is a skilled Lapidary and knows exactly where to cut and how much pressure to apply. He will use every heavenly tool at His disposal to reshape you for His glory—a glory that only *you* can fulfill.

A GEMSTONE IN THE MAKING

This picture of the Master Lapidary was birthed after spending many hours at my (Jim's) lapidary desk contemplating the best design for various rough stones. There are about 15 basic gemstone designs with countless variations of each. You've seen many of them—round brilliants, rectangular "emerald" cuts, square "princess" cuts, triangles, and ovals. Before I select a design, the natural stone must be thoroughly examined to locate its internal defects. The location and shape of the defects greatly influence my choice of design for each stone.

In this chapter we'll peek inside a natural stone so you can see what I see—the birthmarks and blemishes that prevent the release of light—and learn how these influence the design of each stone. The spiritual analogies will quickly become apparent.

Before we begin, let's lay the foundation: Do you know what makes a gemstone valuable; in other words, what makes a precious stone precious? A stone's value hinges on four qualities that collectively determine how well it reflects light. Gemologists call these qualities the "four C's":

- ♦ Color
- ♦ Clarity
- ♦ Carat
- ♦ Cut

Color refers to the hue of the finished stone and its saturation. *Clarity* describes the transparency of the stone. *Carat* is a weight of a stone measured in grams. *Cut* assesses the quality of the lapidary's work for the specific shape or design of the stone. Each stone is graded by these four parameters. A perfect blend of the four ensures sparkling brilliance with the final polish. *Birthmarks* and *blemishes* are two criteria established by The Gemological Institute of America (GIA) to describe flaws that affect the clarity of a gem. *Birthmarks* are defects that form within a crystal during its early growth, or they include fractures that rupture and propagate as the stone is tossed about and battered in a streambed. *Blemishes* are surface defects—"scuffs" that roughen the surface or "frosted" areas that keep light from entering the stone. Both defects reduce a natural stone's clarity by hindering light from entering the stone or preventing the light from reflecting out. Birthmarks and blemishes must be removed, but first "you gotta find 'em!"

LOOKING INSIDE—THE BLUEPRINT OF DESIGN

In college, my favorite course was Optical Mineralogy, the study of mineral properties beneath a powerful research microscope. I'd rush to class, toggle the microscope lamp, adjust the focus knob on the microscope and peer into a world best described as a multicolored kaleidoscope of interlocking shapes. Each shape was either a tiny crystal or a sand grain—the tiny remnant of a former crystal. The intense light and powerful magnification exposed each grain's interior with its fractures, color zonations, bubbles, tiny inclusions of other minerals, and twinning. They reduced the *clarity* of the stone and hindered the passage of light.

Now, multiply a sand grain's size by thousands of times, remove most of the impurities, and saturate it with a rich, constant color and you have a potential piece of gemstone rough. Each piece of rough is a huge, single grain—a former crystal—and, as you might guess, every piece has at least a few imperfections.

Choosing the best design for a complex piece of rough is a challenge, especially if it has strong color orientation and several flaws. Everything hinges on a rigorous examination of the stone's interior.

How do you peek inside? Here's the process I follow:

First, I carefully grip the rough nodule with a pair of long, slender mineral tweezers, adjust my magnifying head visor, and position a strong white light about six inches over a white paper on my desk. The intense light and white surface are essential to display the side of the stone with the strongest color. Next, I attempt to focus past the stone's surface and deep into its interior. Surface blemishes often interfere and cloud the view. Sometimes I'll polish a small area on the rough surface as a window to peek inside. I've polished up to five windows on one sapphire.

Peering into a stone is like entering a strange new world. This is my best attempt to describe the experience:

Visualize a deep swimming pool filled with water on a bright summer afternoon. You don a diver's mask, lay stomach-down alongside the pool's edge, and look beneath the surface. Imagine the beauty of the crystal clear, blue-toned water against the white bottom of the pool. As you look around, you see objects in the water. A silver nickel lies on the bottom of the pool. To the left, a water-sogged tennis ball hangs suspended beneath the surface. Directly under you is a ten-inch crack in the wall of the pool in need of repair. Finally, some distance away and to the right, you see a wispy image—the dangling end of a white cord securing a float.

Congratulations! You've just mapped the birthmarks in a nodule of precious, light-blue aquamarine. It's a journey into another world but it's also a trip into the stone's history. Each flaw, like the object in our swimming pool analogy, tells a story.

A lapidary must identify and map the major flaws to visualize the best shape for the stone. The final design of a cut stone hinges on the shape of the lesser-flawed material. The lapidary must match it with the closest-shaped geometric pattern. If, for example, the least-flawed material is football shaped, then an oval pattern might be selected. If it's long and slender, a rectangular or emerald design would be best.

Fine, precious rough is phenomenally rare and stunningly priced. Large, richly colored tanzanite and tourmaline can exceed $250 per carat. (A carat is a weight measure of 0.2 grams—about twice the size of a spherical capital "O" in this text.) High-quality emerald, sapphire, or alexandrite can be sold for a price many times higher. These prices are for rough, uncut stone. About 60-70% of the stone is cut away with most designs. With such expense, this is why the lapidary must study the flaws in the stone carefully, because the location of the flaws enables him to make the most efficient use of the unflawed portion.

It is impossible to remove all the birthmarks. Natural stones have many inclusions. Tiny birthmarks are left behind because they are valuable—they demonstrate the gem's authenticity as a natural stone. For example, a Columbian emerald *must* possess its diagnostic inclusions to demonstrate authenticity.

The birthmarks in a nodule of rough do not affect the value of the future gem—the flaws will all be ground and polished away by the skilled lapidary. Hopefully, though, you now see how flaws can influence the stone's design. Now it's time to leap to our spiritual analogy and understand the commonalities between the physical birthmarks and blemishes in a natural stone and the spiritual birthmarks and blemishes in us as living stones.

MAPPING SPIRITUAL BIRTHMARKS AND BLEMISHES

In previous chapters we discussed how God originally formed men and women in the protective matrix of His love and how, through the temptation of Satan and our own disobedience, we broke away from the Rock and tumbled into darkness. We ended up in the streambed of life—a sin-dominated world governed by Satan in which his influence and our choices create deep birthmarks within us. Let's look at two types of birthmarks that occur in most living stones:

Formative birthmarks: This type of spiritual birthmark is inherent from birth and becomes more pronounced with each passing year. It's a deeply embedded flaw we possess through what theologians call our "sin nature." At conception, for example, a child may inherit genetic traits that favor addictions such as alcohol abuse. Regardless of our genetic disposition, we are all born with weaknesses and flaws and a rebellious nature. Have you ever heard the saying, "My child is in the 'terrible twos'"? That screaming toddler "pitchin' a fit" and rolling around on the kitchen floor in fanatic disobedience to his parent is simply displaying the flaw of "self-centeredness," embedded within him because of his sin nature.

Situational birthmarks: A second type of birthmark arises from emotional wounds received in the streambed of life. These wounds, left unattended, can manifest years later in self-destructive and harmful behaviors. Consider these examples:

- A twelve-year-old boy opens the door to lust by viewing pornography. Later in life this unrestrained lust causes him to commit adultery against his wife.
- A ten-year-old girl is sexually abused. Low self-esteem and self-worth plague her as an adult.
- A seven-year-old watches her brother die of cancer. Death's terror permeates her thinking throughout her high school years.
- A young boy is told repeatedly by his parents he will never amount to anything. As a middle-aged businessman he drives and crushes his employees in order to succeed at any cost.
- A young woman in her twenties learns she will never conceive children. She dies a bitter woman in a nursing home.

These fractures occur at the moment of abuse, tragedy, or crisis. In each example, the fractures expand and propagate and, with time, create fissures of fear, anger, resentment, or hopelessness. These are the birthmarks—formative or situational flaws that fester and propagate until they reach the surface and shatter the delicate gem.

Now let's consider the second type of spiritual flaw that corrupts the clarity of a living stone: blemishes.

Blemishes are flaws of self-centeredness that cloud our souls and keep the light of Christ from shining forth in our life. Remember our glowing stone in the last chapter? The light shone forth because it emanated from a transparent and humble heart—a heart receptive and focused upon God. In contrast, a heart focused on "self" restricts the penetration and emission of light; pride and selfish ambition are "self's" common traits.

As Jana and I reflect back on our lives, it is apparent that God has diligently labored to remove serious birthmarks and blemishes from each of us. Jana will share how a physical birthmark on her face was actually related to a spiritual birthmark in her soul that created fractures in her self-worth. Then I'll share about how the blemish of "self" kept me from reflecting the light of Christ.

JANA'S BIRTHMARK OF ABANDONMENT
Wham!

I (Jana) slammed the mirror down on the doctor's desk. "Why can't it be removed today?" Tears welled up in my eyes. I wanted to be rid of this hideous birthmark now.

When I looked in the mirror, the obnoxious dark brown patch under my chin screamed, "Look at me!" It made me feel freakish, flawed. Schoolmates sometimes pointed to the mark and asked what was wrong with me. My father made cruel jokes about the ugly birthmark. His remarks fueled my belief that I'd never be pretty enough or good enough for him. Deep down, I hoped if the birthmark was gone he might love me.

In a few weeks I'd start junior high school in a new town. I wanted a fresh start and a fresh "unmarked" face. But it seemed I'd have to live with this mark for another seven days because that was as soon as the doctor could fit me into his surgery schedule. Seven days…one hundred sixty-eight hours…ten thousand eighty minutes. To a teenager, it felt like eternity.

Finally the day arrived. I lay on a cold, hard bed in the center of a freezing, white room with surgical lamps pointing at my chin. Brilliant white light illuminated the hated dark patch. Nervous anticipation caused me to chatter nonstop.

"What are you doing with that needle? Will the numbing shot hurt? What are you gonna do with that knife? If you don't get it all, will it come back?"

"Stop talking and hold still!" the doctor commanded in a stern voice.

I obeyed. It was the first time the kind doctor had spoken harshly to me, and I knew he meant business. As he worked, I felt pressure upon my chin but no pain. Suddenly, his brow arched. Concern filled his eyes. He put the knife on a tray, walked away and asked someone to page Mother on the phone. I heard only his side of the conversation. It sounded serious. The next thing I remembered was waking up in a small room feeling weird—nauseous, loopy-headed, and disoriented.

"Ah, she's awake," the doctor said, as he walked to my bedside in the recovery room. He stood erect, shoved his hands deep into the pockets of his white medical jacket, and spoke to me in a serious tone.

"Jana, the birthmark was not superficial as I had originally thought." Then he spread his hand and fingers under his chin and jaw to demonstrate his next comment. "The birthmark ran deep, intermingled with nerves and bone." His fingers curled, suggesting that the birthmark had grabbed on to other parts of my body.

He paused a moment and then said matter-of-factly, "The cells might be precancerous."

It took a moment for my brain to register his words.

"Cancer? Me?" I responded.

"Probably not. I'm more concerned about possible nerve damage."

In the days that followed I awaited the verdict: Cancer—yes or no? Paralysis—yes or no? Had I endured this surgery only to cause a worse disfigurement or an inability to move my facial muscles? How would my father view me if I had a crooked smile or, even worse, if I lost my hair because of cancer treatments?

In the end, I was fortunate. My birthmark proved noncancerous. I experienced no numbness or paralysis. The doctor removed in one afternoon the physical birthmark that had crushed my self-esteem for years. But the birthmark was merely a physical symbol of a deeper emotional birthmark that marred my young soul—the fractures of abandonment and unfulfilled parental love.

My father left our home when I was a baby. Physical abandonment by him and emotional abandonment by Mother led to my childhood conclusion that I was ugly, dirty, and bad—no one could love me.

The fracture propagated as I matured.

I masked the huge hole in my heart with distrust, self-reliance, people-pleasing works, anger, fear, shame, and a deplorable self-image. As a young wife I tried to prove my worth by doing good works. I must be good, independent, take charge of anything, please everyone and attain perfection. As a young mother, I developed a "super mom" mentality and would trust or depend on no one. In turn, I demanded perfection from my husband and children. My judgmental and self-righteous attitude towards others exhausted me and those closest to me.

In retrospect, secretly I'd hoped that the removal of my physical birthmark would heal my emotional birthmarks of the pain of abandonment by my parents. That did not happen. Instead, the Master Lapidary worked for years to replace the lie that I was ugly, bad, and unlovable and exchange it with the truth that He sees me as beautiful, worthy, and lovable. He also removed the self-preservation mechanisms I once clung to. Removal of my birthmarks required a change in my identity—one focused upon Christ rather than on a job title or the labels others gave me. This is something He has established over the last ten years and continues to solidify within me each day.

JIM'S BLEMISH OF SELF-TRUST

As the son of a tough, Central Texas rancher, my dad's persona reflected a modern-day John Wayne. Like the legendary movie hero's character, hard work and a leather-tough, no-nonsense attitude set the norm. A clear message emerged at an early age: *Hard work makes a man successful.* Later, a more perverted view emerged: In order to gain my father's approval, or anyone's approval, I must work hard. Although some might suggest that my view resulted from the birthmark of conditional love, it manifested within me as the blemish of self-centered responsibility. I carried this distorted thinking to church and applied it to God. God expects me to work for Him and not sin—only then could I make Him happy and earn my way to heaven.

This perverted view of self-responsibility through hard work became my mantra. It perpetuated every task I undertook throughout high school and college.

And it worked!

Grants, awards, recognitions, scholarships and, most importantly, praise came because of my focused efforts. Eventually, though, the positive virtue of self-responsibility degraded into a coarse and frosted smudge of self-reliance and self-trust.

This may not seem like such a horrible flaw but let me show you where it leads.

My attitude of self-reliance and hard work mushroomed after the births of our daughters. I took pride in my ability to provide for all their financial needs. I also took pride in my work. I had to outrank my peers—and I knew what it took to be the best at my job. Long hours away from home each day morphed into weeks away on business trips. After all, it was fully about my performance. I was a valued employee because I put in the time to get the job done. I trusted God to come alongside and bless my efforts, but, in truth, it was up to me to earn the results. I soared in my job on billowing clouds of success while my relationship with Jana became distant and strained.

Eventually, God stepped in to preserve our marriage and polish away my blemish of self-reliance and misplaced trust. How? He allowed my job to end.

The early 1990s saw a dramatic downturn in the oil industry. Huge layoffs and regional office closures became a common theme. *They're just clearing out the deadwood and marginal performers, and the Lord knows there are plenty of those around. I'll be okay.*

Arrogantly, I assumed the cuts would never affect a high performer like me, but the layoffs kept coming; eventually, they caught up with this "high performer."

For the first time in my life I was without a job.

A few months later we moved to a "guaranteed" job in Alaska, which fell through while we were in transit. Now, alone and helpless in Alaska, God carried me through a year of unemployment as I watched every scrap of our family savings evaporate into the cold, dry air. Desperately, I applied for all jobs. Any job. Anywhere. Repeatedly I was turned down. "Over educated," they said. "Over qualified." "You'd become bored and leave in two weeks." I even applied at the local power and electric company to assist digging power line post holes in the frozen Alaska soil. *After all, I'd grown up digging post holes on a Texas ranch. Surely I was qualified for this job.* But the management joked how "smart college types" didn't know what real work was all about.

Finally, broken and helpless, no cash resources, and facedown on the floor in hopeless despair, I realized that it had all been about me… my education, my talents, my abilities to provide. My self-reliant attitude had quenched God's light. It took a full year for the Master Lapidary to polish away my blemishes of self-trust and reposition my focus on Him. At my lowest point He clearly revealed that He is the True Provider, not me. God showed me that every job is a blessing from Him. It's not something I deserve through my own effort. My role is to trust Him, to trust His grace and power alone, not mine. It is up to Him to sustain my family and me.

Do you see how spiritual birthmarks fester and propagate and how blemishes of self hinder the brilliant light of Christ from shining forth? Do you see why the flaws must be identified and removed? For decades God patiently ground away our deep, emotional scars. The process is rough but the results are rewarding as we more clearly reflect His light.

BIRTHMARKS AND BLEMISHES

Do you desire for the light of Christ to shine unhindered in you? If so, you must allow Him to expose the roots of your own deep wounds or sinful habits. Some wounds are apparent; others are so deeply buried that you aren't even aware they exist.

This is where the Master Lapidary steps in. He lowers His visor and carefully beams the powerful light of Christ deep into our inner soul. He focuses past our rough, abraded surface. He peers within and maps the birthmarks and blemishes that plague us. His penetrating look is for one purpose alone—not to violate us or terrify us but to expose the flaws so He might remove them and that we might be filled with His light.

THE EYES OF JESUS

In the book of Revelation, John has a vision in which He records a breathtaking image of Jesus in heaven as our ascended and glorified Lord. John writes, "His face was like the sun shining in its strength" and "His eyes were like a flame of fire."[2] John states that "the Son of God, whose eyes are like a flame of fire,"[3] examined the deeds of the church in Thyatira. He saw their good works and noted them:

> I know your deeds, and your love and faith and service and perseverance, and that your deeds of late are greater than at first.[4]
>
> He also saw their flaws:
>
> I know your deeds...that you tolerate the woman Jezebel, who calls herself a prophetess, and she teaches and leads My bondservants astray....[5]

The church at Thyatira had a problem—they tolerated sin. Jesus told the Thyatira church, "I am He who searches the minds and

77

hearts."[6] His piercing eyes of flame exposed their sin and the individual(s) involved.

Jesus' words reveal a solid truth: All things are seen by Him, both the good and the bad. Nothing is hidden from His sight. Hebrews 4:13 (NLT) says it like this:

> Nothing in all creation can hide from him. *Everything is naked and exposed before his eyes.* This is the God to whom we must explain all that we have done.
> (Emphasis ours.)

Aren't you glad that Jesus sees you, that He observes your devotion, your dedication, your prayers, and your good intentions? The thought comforts us. But it's also unnerving to know that He sees every flaw—every weakness, struggle, fear, pain, and torment—and that He observes these "fractures" even more clearly than we see them ourselves.

The Bible records several interesting accounts from Jesus' earthly ministry where He mysteriously "looks" into the hearts of individuals and exposes what lies within, both the favorable and the unfavorable. Let's consider two of these examples and see how each man in these stories responds to Jesus' scrutiny.

THE BIRTHMARK OF A RICH YOUNG RULER

Just look at the crowded streets. It's difficult to even cross them since the one they call "The Great Teacher" entered our village. People flock to this man. Some want healing. Some want forgiveness. Me? I need a question answered—a very important question.[7] And He just may know the answer. I have to reach Him before He leaves town.

The young man with rings on his fingers and swathed in silk pressed through the throng of humanity with an urgency that caused the crowd to part. He elbowed past poor beggars, mothers holding children, and Pharisees draped in religious robes. He could see the

Teacher now, His hand upon the head of a young boy whom He was blessing. He sidestepped a woman, perhaps the child's mother, and broke into the open space around Jesus. Then he sensed a Divine presence and he did something that surprised himself.

He dropped to his knees in the dirt.

What is it about this man? Even though I've never met Him I recognize His spirit. He possesses authority—and something more. He's not like other leaders who gain position through corruption. This man is innocent. Yes. He can answer my question.

"Good Teacher, what must I do to inherit eternal life?" the young ruler asked.[8]

The restless crowd immediately grew quiet. They, too, wanted to know the answer to this question.

"Why do you call Me good?" Jesus replied with a hint of amusement. "No one is good except God alone."[9]

But Teacher, You are good—maybe even holy… I sense it. Do You imply by Your statement that because You are "good" You are God?

Jesus pulled the man to his feet and spoke loudly, as if addressing the crowd as well as the young ruler before him. "You know the commandments, DO NOT MURDER, DO NOT COMMIT ADULTERY, DO NOT STEAL, DO NOT BEAR FALSE WITNESS, DO NOT DEFRAUD, HONOR YOUR FATHER AND MOTHER.'"[10]

The ruler nodded in agreement. "Teacher, I have kept all of these things from my youth up."[11]

Jesus paused. He turned his attention from the crowd and focused intently on the young man. Heaven and earth collided in a brief flash. The young man's heart beat wildly. Time stopped as the probing eyes of the Great Teacher peered deeply into his very soul—and Jesus perceived completely.

"And *looking* at him, Jesus felt a love for him…"[12] (emphasis ours).

79

Jesus saw this man's desire to love and serve God and He rejoiced. But He saw something else as well, a fracture—a deep, extensive birthmark that occurred as a child—the fracture of false security that comes with affluence and the inheritance of wealth. His possessions kept him from reflecting the full light of God.

"One thing you lack," Jesus said quietly to the man. "Go and sell all you possess, and give to the poor, and you shall have treasure in heaven; and come, follow me."[13]

The young man hung his head.

Do You know how wealthy I am? Do You understand what You are asking of me? It would take years for me to dispense of all my riches. How can You ask me to give up the only way of life that I know?

And he went away grieved, for *he was one who owned much property.*[14]

As we consider this story, we believe two valuable insights can be gleaned from Jesus' "look" and His exchange with the young ruler.

The Lord sees the good in each heart. Scripture makes it clear that when Jesus "looked" at the man His first response was to feel love for him. Clearly, at some level, the young ruler possessed a genuine desire to honor God. The Lord identified a glow in the core of this young, rough nodule and His heart swelled with love—a love that caused Him to take an even deeper look into his soul—a love that led Him to identify the birthmark that prevented the young man from fully reflecting the light of God.

The Lord identifies birthmarks for our benefit. Jesus observed the young ruler's good traits, but He also identified the deceptive darkness of wealth. This birthmark choked his very relationship with God. Jesus said, "…and the deceitfulness of wealth chokes the Word" (Matthew 13:22). Confidence in riches can easily corrupt our faith in God. Jesus' command to "sell all you possess" was not a flippant response to the rich in general, but a strategic action that would grind away this deep flaw in the young man's life so that the light within him could shine unhindered.

This is our first observation of Jesus' penetrating look. Now let's consider another example, one that highlights one of our favorite apostles—a favorite because we relate to his rash and unpredictable nature.

THE BLEMISH OF A WEEPING APOSTLE

We love Peter. When flying high on the wings of self-fueled spontaneity, none soared higher. When crashing under the weight of the ridiculous comment, none landed harder. We wonder, what drove Peter's outspoken nature? Was it a courageous "snub your nose" attitude toward death? Or was it a deep craving for acceptance—a crushing need to please people by saying what he thought others wanted to hear?

Jesus' first encounter with Peter was memorable. Half-naked and smelling of day-old mackerel, Peter knew all about fishing. His hands were hard and calloused from pulling in loaded nets. But this self-reliant, tough fisherman possessed a sensitive spirit towards the things of God. He threw aside his nets so that he could follow Jesus and become "a fisher of men."

Over the course of the next three years, we can only imagine how many times Jesus peered into Peter's heart, this muscled man who would shoulder responsibility for establishing His church in Judea and beyond. Spontaneous, outspoken, and self-confident, Peter exhibited true zeal for His Lord. But what flaws resided within? Jesus knew, and He gave us a hint the night of His betrayal.

Jerusalem bustled with excitement as scores of family and friends gathered in homes to celebrate a sacred meal—the Feast of Unleavened Bread. Jesus and his disciples reclined around a large table laden with matzah, charoset, boiled potatoes, roasted lamb, and wine. The atmosphere in the room swung from excitement to distress as Jesus announced that he was going to be put to death by the Jewish leaders. Even more startling, Jesus revealed that His betrayer sat at His very table. The disciples were dumbfounded. After all, Jesus was the Messiah! He'd come to save the people, to deliver them from their oppressors, not to die for them.

A few hours later, Jesus made another inconceivable announcement that, this very night, "...you [the disciples] will all fall away on account of me."[15] The idea seemed ludicrous. Peter boastfully declared, "Even though all may fall away, yet I will not."[16] Jesus knew Peter's heart. He contradicted the disciple with words that surely seemed impossible: "Before a cock crows twice, [you] shall three times deny me."[17]

A few hours passed, and suddenly, Peter's world hung upside down. His Lord stood a stone's throw away. Jewish guards and angry onlookers spit in His face, slapped Him and pounded Him with their fists. Peter heard each slap and winced as if he'd been the one struck. All the while questions assaulted his mind.

Why doesn't He do something instead of just standing there? I've seen Him stop the waves of a raging sea—twice! I've seen Him renounce religious zealots; why doesn't He defend Himself? I would rescue Him, but what can I do against this crazed crowd?

And then, accusations were hurled *at him*, "You, too, were with Jesus"..."This is one of them"..."Surely you *are* one of them...a Galilean."[18] Peter denied each claim and eventually cursed and swore, "I do not know this man you are talking about!"[19]

A rooster's raucous crow pierced the chilly morning.

Then Scripture states, "And the Lord turned and *looked* at Peter. And Peter remembered the word of the Lord...And he went out and wept bitterly"[20] (emphasis ours).

Again, the text offers two valuable lessons from the "look" of Jesus and the reaction of the grieving apostle.

The "look" of Jesus exposes self. Peter had followed Jesus for three years. He'd seen Him heal the blind and resurrect the dead. Peter himself had, in the power of Jesus' name, healed the sick and cast out demons. He'd witnessed the transfigured Lord speaking with Moses and Elijah. And still, Peter's blemish of self-reliance drove him to brash actions. He refused to surrender self until the depths of its wickedness were fully exposed. His arrogant boast, "I will never fall away"...his three denials...the rooster's crow...and finally, the look from His abused Lord. These events erected the grand stage of Providence designed to expose Peter's foolish reliance on self and teach Him to trust God.

The "look" of Jesus brings repentance. When Jesus looked at Peter it not only exposed the residues of self but it cut deeply into Peter's soul. Andrew Murray wrote of the scene:

> ...then the Lord looked upon him; and that look of Jesus broke the heart of Peter, and all at once there opened up before him the terrible sin that he had committed, the terrible failure that had come, and the depth into which he had fallen...Oh! Who can tell what that repentance must have been?[21]

It only takes a glance from "eyes like a flame of fire" to convict those who love the Lord but who, because of their self-centered ways, stumble. Peter's tenuous faith and self-centered tendencies were fully exposed that morning in a way he surely never forgot.

UP CLOSE AND PERSONAL

We gleaned four valuable principles from these two stories: The Lord sees the good in every heart; He exposes our birthmarks in an attempt to bring healing in our lives; He looks deep into our souls in order to expose our selfish ways; and when we see our selfishness we repent, which realigns our heart with God's heart.

It's all about that look. Jesus *must* look. His love demands it. But we must be willing to look as well, to see what He sees, and allow Him to remove what He must.

Will you do that now? Will you give Jesus permission to look upon your own soul, to expose what you cannot see? If you are so brave, then devote some time to walk through these four simple steps based on verses in Psalm 139.

BELIEVE: Believe that Jesus knows every cell in your body, every situation you've experienced, every dream you've imagined, every disappointment you've experienced. Believe that He has a plan for your life and that He will use everything in your life for His good purposes. Meditate on Psalm 139:15 and 16:

> My frame was not hidden from you when I was made in the secret place. When I was woven together in the depths of the earth. *Your eyes saw my unformed body*; all the days ordained for me were written in your book before one of them came to be.
>
> (Emphasis ours.)

ASK: Ask the Lord to search everything in your heart and to reveal any situation in which you need to receive or offer forgiveness. Say out loud these verses from Psalm 139:23 and 24:

> Search me, God, and know my heart; test me and know my anxious thoughts. See if there is any offensive way in me, and lead me in the way everlasting.

CONFESS: Confess, or "agree with," any situation God brings to your mind. Talk to Him in prayer. You could pray something like this:

Oh Lord, all of my life I've struggled with _____.
You understand its source and how deeply its roots run.
Please examine my life and identify my birthmarks and
blemishes. Remove these flaws and restore me to the
image and design You had in mind at creation. I trust
You, Holy God, to use everything in my life to glorify You
and to bring praise to Your name.

RECEIVE: Receive the love of God. Allow His love and light to flood your heart and fill your being so that you might rejoice and praise Him for the amazing way He created you.

Even the darkness will not be dark to you; the night will
shine like the day... I will praise you because I am fear-
fully and wonderfully made; your works are wonderful, I
know that full well.
(Ps. 139: 12, 14, emphasis ours)

Finally, dwell on the splendor of God's plans. Isaiah 55:8 and 9 says, "For my thoughts are not your thoughts, neither are your ways my ways," declares the LORD. "As the heavens are higher than the earth, so are my ways higher than your ways and my thoughts than your thoughts."

Aren't you glad that nothing you can imagine for your own life is as great as the plans God has in mind for you?

GEMS 2

PRAYER:

Lord, I BELIEVE that You know me intimately and have great plans for me. I ASK You to search my heart for offensive ways and for the wounds which hinder my walk in Your Kingdom. Lord, I CONFESS that I have flaws and I need Your healing touch. I am helpless to help myself. And Lord, I RECEIVE Your tender love and ask that Your light flood my soul and change me back into the image You had in mind to begin with.

God knows me intimately and will remove everything that distorts His image.

- Early trauma in our past influences our current behaviors and attitudes.
- Birthmarks are deep-seated flaws in our nature from wounds that were often beyond our control.
- Blemishes are the smudges of "self" that include pride and self-reliance.
- Jesus' "look" reveals the "good" and exposes the birthmarks in each soul.
- His "look" also exposes self and brings repentance.

CHAPTER

Never Let Go

"**I** WILL NOT LET go. I will not let go." My fingers pressed deep into Jenny's small, icy-wet wrist. I squeezed with all my strength.

The sound of my pounding heart overpowered the horror-stricken screams from across the creek as I repeated, "I will not let go. *I will not let go!*"

Two hours north of Anchorage and miles from civilization, the Willow Creek flows into the illustrious Susitna River. On this rainy Saturday in July, we and another family crammed into our Suburban and headed out to catch our limit of wild Alaskan salmon where the rivers joined.

The rain didn't dampen our spirits, nor had it kept away the tourists. Hundreds of people crowded shoulder to shoulder along the creek banks zealously casting their lines. "Combat fishing" received its name from these types of fishermen-infested banks. Our family preferred to hike upstream away from the crowds. To reach our hidden location, we had to cross multiple tributaries through bear-infested woods. Broad, Cheshire-cat grins beamed across our faces as we hiked past the crowds on our way to our private fishing hole.

We each packed a load of stuff. "Sourdoughs," seasoned Alaskans, recognize that backwoods excursions require proper equipment and supplies. On previous trips we'd used our emergency provisions to remove embedded hooks, suture cuts, splint broken bones and soothe a chicken pox outbreak. Necessary items included extra clothes, fire starters, bear protection—a gun and pepper spray—and food and water.

Then there's the fishing gear. Salmon fishing gear is awkward and heavy, *especially* on a long walk through dense woods.

We wore our waders while hiking to help keep dry, but they made for awkward and difficult movements. This Texas city gal had never heard of waders until moving to Alaska. I certainly didn't know the difference between hip and chest waders. Hip waders, I quickly learned, are bulky, oversized rubber boots which extend over your knees and halfway up your thighs, with straps that snap to the belt loops on your jeans. They're perfect for long-legged folks, but for stubby-legged people like me, one misstep can fill our boots with icy glacier water. Me? I go for chest waders every time.

"Going on a lion hunt, I'm not afraid... Through the woods..." We sang at the top of our voices for bear alert. We paused only to spit out an occasional mosquito or climb over a fallen tree.

And to listen...

Drip, drop, splat! *Sluuurrrppppp.* Synchronized raindrops beat the foliage drums. With each step the sticky, slimy mud sucked at our boots to create rhythmic backwoods harmony. A distant *bang!* from park rangers setting off firecrackers to shoo grizzly bears away from the crowds added a symbol crash to the rhythm.

Bang, bang... KaBoom! We stopped. *Whew! That one was close.*

Hmm. We were in the woods, away from the crowds. What if the fireworks had scared the bear in our direction? We listened. We looked. We waited.

"Do you think we should turn back?" Jim voiced our unspoken concerns as we speculated which direction the bear ran.

We took a quick look around.

"Nawww. Nothing will stop us," we agreed. Not a bear on the run, nor his large tracks that we had stepped over at the last stream. Not the fresh scat still steaming in the light rain. No, we had fish on the brain and dreams of a full freezer. Some would say we're crazy; others know it's the Alaskan way.

Two hours later we cast our first hooks into the turbulent stream. The two youngest girls danced around in the smoke from our small fire sizzling on a sandbar. The girls squealed and laughed; we looked up, smiled, and cast again. I cast and cast, concentrating on every bump of the line. I knew the "feel" of the bottom as my weight bounced along with the current.

Wham! My fly rod bent in half.

"Fish on!" I yelled. *Oh, oh, it feels like a big one. Remember to palm the reel. Oh yeah, not too hard. Don't let him take too much line.*

"Keep your tip up! Turn his nose," Jim instructed as he rushed over with the net. "That's the way... play him until he tires out." The monster leapt from the water.

"Fish on," yelled Julie, our oldest daughter, a few yards away.

Ten hours later, exhausted, sore, and fished out, we surveyed our bounty of 60 pounds of salmon filets. Smiles all round *until* we lifted the additional weight to pack back to the car—like adding five bowling balls to our load.

"What's that smell?" one of the girls asked.

"Us," I laughed. *Oh great. We reek of fish. We've become bear magnets.* Alaskans don't use flashlights in the summer because we are the "land of the midnight sun." But this day the dim light from the overcast evening quickly slipped away and, combined with the dreary drizzle, created miserable trail conditions. Jim led the way in search of the best way out. Often the trail was impassible.

Another backtrack, I inwardly moaned. Exhausted we turned around and forged onward along a different route.

Jim continually banged two sticks together for bear alert because we were too tired to sing the bears away. The young girls and I lagged further and further behind. One foot slipped out from under me; the next step, sticky mud tried to suck the wader off my leg.

"Mom, help!"

"Mom, I'm cold."

"Mom, I'm tired." Frustrated cries came every few yards. The rain increased.

We redistributed my gear among the adults so I could assist the younger girls and get them back to the car faster. Able to move at a quicker pace, the three of us forged about 200 yards ahead of the group. *Light!* An open grass field lay ahead.

"Yeah! We're almost there," I chimed as the girls and I stepped out of the dense woods...but not out of danger.

One last stream to cross.

Goose bumps raced across my body. Tall thick grass rose well above my head.

My eyes strained to see any movement along the top of the grass knowing that grizzlies could be nearby. We were alone and unarmed. My heart raced. My nerves sprang to attention. I grabbed the girls' hands. *Should we wait for the others or go on?*

"Mom, I gotta go to the bathroom." Jenny broke the silence. We could see the other side of the bank lined with fishermen (and women). *I think it will be okay. We are so close.* The steady rain and rushing creek hindered my ability to hear any other sound. Against my instincts, we trudged on. The girls picked up the pace in anticipation of a warm car. Their muddy boots slid across the fallen wet grass like dancers across the stage. Jenny did a pirouette, fell in a hole, and landed in the mud. Unconcerned and unaware, both girls laughed and horsed around.

We must get out of here! I knew most bear encounters occurred in this section.

"Girls, pay attention and stop fooling around," I commanded brusquely. My heightened awareness intensified every movement. The trail followed dangerously close beside the creek yet provided a sense of security with the new visibility.

"Step here," I pointed and shouted over the sound of the creek. In turn, the one behind me repeated the motion and instruction.

"Fish on!" someone hollered from across the creek. Shouts of excitement drew my attention. Then another shout, not of excitement, but of fear.

"Noooooo!"

Splash!

I'm not sure which I heard first, the scream from the woman across the creek or the loud splash. Instinctively I turned towards the hysterical woman. Her outstretched arm pointed to the deep swift water that separated us. I looked around.

Where's Jenny? Panic. My stomach churned. She was nowhere in sight. Rapidly I scanned the bank where the lady pointed. Where? Where?

There!

Jenny's tiny fingertips clung to the edge of the grassy bank, her body completely submerged beneath the swiftly moving water as her waders became lead stockings and pulled her ever deeper. I lunged to grab her, and in an instant my feet went out from under me. I fell facedown in the slimy mud. More screams, this time mine. Crawling, slipping, screaming.

"Jenny! *Jenny!*"

Somehow I reached the edge and grabbed both of her wrists. The woman across the creek continued her hysterical screams. By now others had joined in with loud distorted sounds.

My own thoughts screamed. *No, God… Please help!*

"I will not let go. I will not let go." My fingers pressed deep into her small, icy-wet wrist. I squeezed with all of my strength.

The current tried to rip her from my grip. I tried to gain extra strength by taking a deep breath, but my nose and mouth sucked in more mud.

The sound of my heart overpowered the horror-stricken screams from across the creek.

I will not let go. I will not let go!

Still lying on my stomach, my arms and shoulders stretched taut by the weight of Jenny and her water-filled waders, the swift current began to win the tug-of-war. My fingers began to slip.

Adrenaline? No. Something more. Something supernatural—God. Somehow, in one quick motion I snatched her from the depths of the terrifying water.

Whomp! She plopped out of the water as I rolled over, and then she landed on top of me, face to face on my chest. I hugged her with all of my strength. The impact and my forceful clutch caused her to cough up water all over my grimy face. Simultaneously, a surge of icy water poured over us from her waders. I lay there crying, "I will not let go. I will not let go." Jenny's young friend fell across the top of us crying too, a wad of jumbled, sobbing bodies.

Whew. Safe in my arms.

Jim dashed out of the woods. From the screams, he expected to see a bear attacking his family.

"Ahwww, ahww, ahw," screamed the hysterical woman pointing at the ground in front of him. Jim stopped, cocked his head slightly, looked at the woman and then back down at us. He shook his head in confusion. What a sight. Me, drenched, covered in mud, lying flat on my back. Jenny on my stomach and her friend draped over top of us, all of us crying. The hysterical lady screaming from the other side of the creek. His wife and daughter lying in the nasty muck, soaked. Yet all seemed to be okay.

Calmly he asked, "What's all the commotion? Why are you lying in the mud?"

Jenny and I looked into each other's eyes, turned our faces to the hysteria across the creek, and looked back up at her friend, then at Jim. His perplexed expression caused us to erupt in a fit of uncontrollable laughter.

Weeks later Jenny shared her adventure at the school's Show and Tell. She began her story by saying, "My mom saved my life." She calmly described to the class how being under the cold water took her breath away and how weird it felt to suck in a mouthful of water instead of air. She described how she felt when she could not pull herself up. As a previous swim team member, Jenny knew how long she could hold her breath when she sucked in air. This time she had little breath to hold. Her lungs had taken in water.

"I survived because I focused on the light shining through the water," she explained. "In the light I saw my mom's face, and then I just focused on her. I knew as long as I could see her she would never let go." She did not remember the pressure of my grip as I squeezed her wrists, only my face.

Her calm, matter-of-fact attitude initiated phone calls from parents and her teacher. Each asked me to validate her rendition.

"Was the danger life-threatening?" they wanted to know. Yes.

"Was Jenny really that calm and fearless?" Yes.

Jenny displayed childlike faith and complete trust when totally engulfed by the icy torrent. Hebrews 11:1 (NLT) says "...faith...is the confident assurance that what we hope for is going to happen." Jenny was confident I would save her. As long as she looked at my face she never doubted or questioned.

Two important concepts about faith emerged from that terrifying moment on the Willow Creek bank. First, I was struck by Jenny's childlike faith in me. She looked into my face and trusted, even under the threat of death, that I would save her. This is the kind of childlike faith that God wants from me—to look into His face and trust that, even though turbulent waters swirl around me, nothing can separate me from the love of God...not even a swift river (Romans 8:38, 39).

Second, I discovered that faith involves "holding on," and this holding-on process has marvelous similarities with gemstone fashioning. Our gemstone analogy paints a vivid picture of faith, how it secures us to God's hand and the disastrous consequences of "letting go." I'll bow out for a moment and let Jim explain the process from the lapidary's perspective.

THE DOP—OUR BRASS ROD OF FAITH

A dop, rough stone, and a stick of wax. Seems rather basic doesn't it?

The process of gluing two objects together with hot wax has undoubtedly been around for centuries. Mounting a stone sounds simple until you try it. The challenge of securing a costly piece of precious rough to the end of a brass rod—aligned with the design and fastened so tightly that the stone shifts less than a thousandth of an inch—is just a bit daunting. I've failed more than once!

To begin, I carefully align the stone with the dop using the design criteria. We've discussed the unique nature of each stone and the importance of a proper design. Precise alignment assures the best color in the finished stone and efficient removal of fractures and waste material. Accurate alignment leaves the gem-quality material untouched and properly oriented for the final design.

Once aligned, I glue the stone to the dop. This step, for me, is one of the most challenging of the stone-crafting process. The simple metal rod attaches the stone to the cutting head for guidance by the lapidary's hand. The stone must be *securely* mounted to withstand the pressure of fashioning into a gem. Even the slightest shift changes the angles, distorts the final design, and dulls the reflected light.

The dop is a simple, pencil-like brass rod. It serves the important task of orienting the stone to the exact angles and depths required for cutting and polishing. When attached to the cutting head it becomes an extension of the lapidary's hand and securely holds the stone at the correct angles.

Mounting the stone to the dop is a tricky process. A flat spot is ground on the stone's surface at the precise location. The flat spot is carefully aligned and mounted to the dop with a hard, high-temperature wax. The wax forms a critical joint between the stone and dop. It resembles our faith. The precise amount of heat must be applied to melt the wax and warm the stone; the wax and stone must be hot enough for the wax to "flow." This part is critical—too much heat and the stone may be damaged. Too little heat is just as dangerous; it prevents the wax from curing correctly in the joint's interior. A "cold" (weak) joint will result. It often fails (snaps) during polishing when the pressure is most severe.

Aligned and dopped, the stone is ready to cut. Cutting thrills the lapidary, and I can't wait to begin. The first few cuts unveil the design, as weak flashes of light emerge. Subsequent cuts shape the facets bit by bit. The process is methodical, satisfying, and soothing. For me, cutting a stone is calming therapy—until the stone flies off the dop.

When that happens "catastrophic" is the best word to describe it. Transformation halted.

The dop instantly slams onto the lap's hard surface. The stone, now free on the spinning lap, either ricochets like a bullet inside the splash rim or is catapulted into the room like a missile. It's a split-second, chaotic event—a violent interruption that may chip, fracture, or even break the stone. So much for soothing therapy!

I know the instant a stone breaks free it must be recut. A stone on the dop may slightly shift, especially during the heat and pressure of polishing. A good lapidary makes subtle corrections called "cheating" to account for the shift, and the effects on the polished gem are generally unnoticeable. But a stone that flies off the dop suffers a different fate.

I diligently search for the errant stone—under the lap, in the carpet, under the rocking chair. And just like a shepherd with a lost sheep, joy and relief come with discovery. But joy fades into nervous concern as I examine the stone for damage.

A chip or fracture is serious and often requires a different design. The refashioned gem reflects light differently than the original pattern; its brilliance and color have changed. Such is the fate of a stone that leaves the dop.

Sometimes an undamaged stone can be reattached along the joint's original broken wax surfaces. Unfortunately, the glue itself changes the alignment and the facets must still be recut. This retains the original design but with a portion of the precious material lost forever.

CRACKS IN THE FAITH-JOINT

"Jump." Jim called to our little girl.

"Catch me, Daddy!" Julie squealed.

One moment a toddler stood perched on the edge of the patio roof, and the next moment she flew through the air into her daddy's arms. Doubt never entered Julie's mind when her daddy placed her on the "really high and scary" place. She focused on her daddy's eyes and jumped. She knew her daddy, trusted him fully, and leapt into his outstretched arms.

How did Julie know her daddy wouldn't drop her or let her go? How did Jenny know I (Jana) wouldn't let go when she was on the verge of drowning? Julie knew her daddy's voice, his face, and his love. Jenny knew my face, my love, and she knew I would do anything to save her. Both girls experienced authentic relationship with us, and, as a result, childlike faith came easily.

Childlike faith in a heavenly Father is easy for some; others, like me, struggle to trust that He will not drop or let go of me. As a young girl I'd shine a flashlight upwards at night through my window and ask, "Are You there, God? Can You see or hear me? Do You love me?" My young, inquisitive mind believed He answered, *Yes*. Initially I possessed a childlike faith, but then I allowed life events to crack and weaken my faith. My questions, "Are You there, God? Can You see or hear me? Do You love me?" seemed to be answered with a resounding, *No*.

The "How?" "Why?" and "What had I done, or not done?" questions haunted me. I earnestly desired to trust God with unhindered faith but couldn't figure it out. Legalistic guilt took root. Hebrews 11:6 says that it is impossible to please God without faith. Since I thought my faith was weak, I believed I was unable to please God.

I eventually realized that when I looked at God's face His image was distorted through years of my own lies, wounds, and pain.

Without realizing it, childhood scars had caused me to question God's Word and develop a misshapen perception of His love and character. Let me share three hazards that "weakened my joint with the dop," which represents my faith.

I DOUBTED GOD'S WORD.

My faith in God developed its first crack when I was ten years of age. We moved from Houston to a small town in Central Texas to be close to my grandparents, and I got to attend church regularly. I received my first Bible and read as much as I could. In my child's mind all was well until one day Mother came home from work and accused me of horrible things I had not done. After several minutes her words turned from condemnation of my behavior to cursing my character and identity. In an instant, I learned to dissociate from emotional and physical pain. Mother believed I was bad and evil and often told me so. When I was eleven years old, she validated her words with violence. Her punishment began with multiple belt lashes. I had witnessed her psychotic rage towards others, but this time it focused on me.

"Cry!" she screamed with each lash.

"You can't make me cry anymore." I sternly replied through gritted teeth.

Mercilessly she beat me across the back, arms, and legs.

"Cry, you will cry! CRY!"

The scene continued until my brother came in and pulled her off of me. Running into my room I fell onto my bed. Welts covered my backside, some open and bleeding. My face landed on my pillow, which hid my open Bible where I had been memorizing a verse for Bible class about God's love and protection. Silent wails escaped through sobs and a flood of tears. Accusations and rage surged through me. *God, You promise in the Bible to fight for me, to be my protector. Where were You when Mom was beating me? Are*

Your words true or just lies? Maybe they're for others and not me. Are You like my 'real' father, whose words are meaningless, and he's never around when I need him? Do You make promises and then allow bad things to happen?

If I couldn't trust what I read in the Bible, then I couldn't trust God. I doubted God's Word because of my distorted perception of truth. The door of doubt opened—a crack in the wax. Mother denied her actions and said she'd call me a liar if I ever mentioned what happened. After a childhood dominated by put-downs, deception, and manipulation, I'd been desensitized to truth.

But it didn't end there. Rejection by others and negative words opened another door of deception. This one led me to question God's love.

I DOUBTED GOD'S LOVE.

Maybe I really was bad, insignificant, and unlovable. Confusion ruled my mind. In church and Bible class I'd hear, "You're special; you're so loved," but, at home I'd experience, "You're worthless; no one cares about you." I prayed and yearned to know God deeper. I wanted His love and to love Him. I sensed God was the answer, but He seemed distant.

Mother married again when I was in the seventh grade. Poof! I had another instant family, a new stepfather and stepbrother, and a new school. However, this time a sliver of hope sparkled. We became like a real family. We did normal things, like family dinners at the table; we had company over; we took a real vacation.

Ray, another of many stepfathers, taught me how to hunt, drive, and the importance of integrity. He showed interest in me and my dreams. He bought a piano and allowed me to take lessons for pure enjoyment. His words and actions seemed to be true and loving. I slowly grew to trust him. He wasn't a Christian but he demonstrated unconditional love. Mother professed to be a Christian but expressed conditional love. It all seemed confusing, but I didn't care, because I now had this new father to trust.

Then he died.

I felt abandoned again. If God loved me, why would He give me something good then take it away? Scared and lonely, I searched for something solid to hang on to. I continued to read my Bible. Maybe if I knew more facts about God I could trust Him.

Sweet sixteen became ugly sixteen. A few months after Ray's death, mother married a man who had been involved in the Mafia (I know this sounds like it is right out of a soap opera, but it *is* true!). Hot on his trail, the FBI descended upon our small Central Texas town. We were the local news. They fingerprinted everything—my school papers, typewriter, and car. An agent followed me to school and to other functions. I felt condemned and banished by the community.

With my brother Hal already in college, mother became more self-absorbed, except for the random, psychotic explosions which usually targeted me. One night, after one of her crazy rages, I fled to the safety of my pastor's home, hoping he and his wife would take me in.

"Go home; you're too young to move out," they said.

Rejected by the church. Maybe I *was* unlovable and horrible like mother constantly said. A few months later mother married Roy, Ray's brother. Their marriage lasted less than two years.

Mother provided a lifetime of unhealthy love and relationship examples—she couldn't live with or without a man. Mother divorced Roy at the beginning of my senior year. She and I moved into an apartment across from the high school. We lived together until the day I came home after school to discover a naked man passed out on the couch. I had to find a safe place. Surely *now* my grandparents would take me in until I finished high school. I packed my suitcase and drove to their country home. My grandfather met me at the door. Mother had called ahead.

"How can you do this to your little momma?" Pa scolded. "You call yourself a Christian and abandon her when she needs you the most. Go home and take care of her. Now get out of here." Pa closed the door.

It must be me. Others believe Mother is good and don't see her like I do. I can't depend on anyone.

Just before my eighteenth birthday I moved out—alone. *Where are You, God? Is this love? Selfish, fleeting, conditional? Am I so bad or dirty no one can love me?*

Mother left town, moved hundreds of miles away, and wanted nothing to do with me. The previous year I'd met and started dating a college man, a Christian, who patiently endured my chaos and desired to love me unconditionally. I didn't know how to receive his gentleness and kept him at arm's length. Would he leave me too? I constantly tested and questioned his love, much like I did God's. And, if you doubt God's love, the One who defines love, how in the world can you understand His character?

I DIDN'T UNDERSTAND GOD'S CHARACTER.

Jim and I married during the spring break of my first year of college. I believed life was now perfect. I had a husband who really loved me. A few years later we were blessed with two wonderful little girls. However, I was terrified of acquiring even a hint of mother's character. In my distorted way of becoming most *unlike* my mother, I became "super-Christian-woman-wife-mom." I believed I could control life and be so good that God and others would love and admire me. Seeking approval for years, I threw myself into busyness and self-gratifying tasks. I believed God was like the adults in my life who judged, pointed out my faults, and criticized my character. In my first Bible I'd underlined and highlighted I Timothy 4:11-16. From these verses I developed a formula for life—a very performance-based life formula:

Be a worthy servant and work hard.

Train for spiritual fitness.

Teach and be an example to all.

Jim and I shared many of the same beliefs about God and the church. We worked hard for God, to prove our faith, only to experience multiple church splits and little brotherly love.

Where was love? Where was God? We questioned the legalistic aspects of religion and decided to leave our church heritage in a desperate search for love and truth. We began attending a Bible church that stressed grace over works—grace-based theology believes that God freely gives His love to us, and there is nothing we can do to earn or deserve that love. Jim was like a sponge, soaking up the newfound doctrine. Me, I was like putty. I could conform to the new teaching but I didn't allow much to penetrate.

Sure ... there were good times. We loved each other and our daughters. We had raised our family in the beautiful and exciting state of Alaska, which resulted in many family adventures. We heard more about God's grace. Still, it seemed everything I thought was important and worked towards failed or let me down. Secretly I continued to question God's Word, His love, and His character. My childlike faith had vanished long ago, and I had no idea how to reclaim it.

During Julie's last and Jenny's first year of high school I became apathetic and essentially stopped reading the Bible and praying. Oh, I still went to church, and outwardly I appeared to be a model Christian, wife, and mother, but inwardly I was at war with myself, as I constantly battled my distorted perceptions of God, family, and self.

Our oldest daughter Julie married. Bored with life, we needed a new distraction, so we decided to add a little more chaos and build a house. We built our home nestled in the mountainous Eagle River Valley, close to the river, in the middle of God's beautiful creation. It was there that God moved and recaptured my full attention.

THE FRAGILE FAITH-JOINT HEALED

Our yard grew rocks and boulders. I wanted grass. After a lot of sweat and money, we had green. Our neighbor's 150-pound Newfoundland—a long-haired, black dog—loved the freshly packed soil and green fuzzy blanket of baby grass to romp, roll, and dig. Early one morning, while drinking coffee and watering the grass, I spotted the beast headed for my baby lawn.

"Shoo, get out of here!" I yelled, as I dropped my coffee cup and charged towards him waving my arms.

"Grrrraaah," growled the "dog," as it stood up on its back legs.

Oops!

Instantly I turned and sprinted in the opposite direction. The black bear did the same.

My husband to this day jokes about that poor bear. He says the bear is now psychotic and probably still on the run, believing that a deranged blonde woman is after him.

Not many people can say, or want to say, they've charged a wild bear. I believed the bear was our neighbor's dog. It was a case of mistaken identity, one that provided a great analogy for my distorted spiritual beliefs. For much of my life, I had mistakenly believed God was like my biological father—absent when needed, or like mother—condemning and unloving. And, like people, I believed God was undependable.

Shortly after his wife's death, C.S. Lewis penned these words: "You never know how much you really believe anything until its truth or falsehood becomes a matter of life and death to you."[1] I was at such a crossroads. If I was ever to recover my childlike faith, I had to exchange God's true identity for the identity I'd assigned Him, based on the wounds of my past. I needed a "face-to-faith" encounter with the True Living God. This happened soon after the bear scare when a major surgery forced me to be housebound for six weeks.

My friends sometimes call me the Energizer® bunny because I'm always on the go, but after the surgery I could hardly move! God forced me into stillness, and I used the quiet time to get to know Him—*really* know Him. I started reading my Bible again. I also spent time in reflection and self-examination, and what I saw frightened me. My soul felt black, lifeless. This came in stark contrast to the images outside my window where the mountain valley exploded with spring color and new life. Tulips and daffodils danced in the breeze. Birch tree leaves shimmered like millions of tiny tambourines. Baby birds and squirrels—in fact the whole hillside—seemed to sing. As I flipped through my Bible, the words from Isaiah 55:12 (NLT) jumped off the page, offering a soundtrack for the landscape musical before me:

"You will live in joy and peace. The mountains and hills will burst into song, and the trees of the field will clap their hands!"

Ahhh, it was as if God and I were having our own little party, as we watched all of nature burst forth in joy. It felt as if He'd orchestrated this dance of nature just for me. In that moment He felt near and oh so trustworthy. He whispered that I was His child... that He adored me. Never before had I experienced such holy love, a pure love that washed over me and demanded nothing in return.

Day after day God poured into me doses of affirmation, love, healing, provision, mercy, and grace. As my body mended so did my spirit. Slowly but firmly, my childlike faith was reborn, as He renewed my heart for more of Him. I began to see that faith is built through intimacy with God, *not* through performance. I'd tried to perform my way into stronger faith. As a result, my faith had become self-focused and weak. Faith requires surrender and trust, not works. I grappled for years with the *whys* and *hows,* instead of just basking in an intimate relationship with my Father.

It was my own personal miracle. In these quiet weeks of recovery I quit twisting and squirming in His lap and came to a place where

I could nestle against His chest and let Him deal with the questions I couldn't answer. Like the Psalmist, my soul declared:

> O LORD, my heart is not proud, nor my eyes haughty;
> *Nor do I involve myself in great matters,*
> *Or in things too difficult for me.*
> Surely I have composed and quieted my soul;
> Like a weaned child rests against his mother,
> My soul is like a weaned child within me.
>
> (Psalm 131:1, 2, emphasis ours)

I wish I could tell you that from that moment forward, I never again wavered in my childlike faith. That wasn't the case. Jenny's death, and all that came with it, fractured my tender faith yet again. But once again, God brought me back to Himself in an encounter that rocked me.

Seven years later, I sat in a chair holding the spotted hand of a frail ninety-one-year-old woman who lay in a bed at a nursing home. Mrs. Howell had ministered to others and served God her whole life. She had "done things" well. She'd suffered terrible evil at the hands of others, yet she still maintained rock-solid faith. How? Her life and words often spoke of knowing God personally and intimately. She knew, really knew, how to just *be*... to be alone and one with God.

I studied her soft, lined face as her chest peacefully rose and fell. Her eyes were closed, and I suspected she was asleep, which gave me a safe sounding board to express the doubts and fears that had resurfaced as a result of Jenny's death. "I had childlike faith once," I cried. "But I don't know how to get it back."

Suddenly Mrs. Howell's eyes popped open. In a clear, strong voice, as if God Himself were speaking to me, she said: "Childlike faith and trust are easy. It's a fact—just believe."

Could it really be that simple? Was it really just a moment-by-moment choice? My mind raced back to Jenny, submerged in the water, as she stared peacefully into my eyes. She trusted me to save her. She didn't know how I'd do that; she just believed I would.

"It's easy. Just believe."

I'm doing that today. When a doubt tugs me in the wrong direction, I push it away with simple belief. Childlike faith is once again capturing my imagination. Probably in the future I'll find myself submerged beneath some swiftly moving river. I want to believe that, instead of letting doubt and fear pull me under, I'll display childlike faith in God, but honestly, I don't know what the future holds. All I can do is make a choice for today. In this moment, I choose to look into my Father's eyes, to hang onto Him, and to simply believe Him when He says, "I won't let go."

2 GEMS

PRAYER:

Dear Father, I believe in You, but I often doubt You because I don't understand Your ways. Increase my faith. Keep Your face before me. Keep me in the palm of Your hand, and help me to trust that You'll never let me go.

God never lets me go—nothing can separate me from His love.

- Believe that God's love is stronger than our doubts or questions.
- Examine and compare your thoughts to God's Word—the Bible.
- Focus on the truth—God's love and faithfulness is never-ending.

CHAPTER

An Emerald, a Green Flash, and a Changed Life

"**D**O YOU BELIEVE the man's story at the restaurant? Do you believe it really could happen?" Jana asked, as she peered intently into the sunbeams glinting off the distant ocean waves.

"I don't know; I guess we'll find out." I (Jim) snuggled against her, as we sat side by side on the white Hawaiian beach. A cool ocean breeze—the harbinger of sunset—rustled the palm fronds overarching the beach. *The comfort of a warm touch of flesh; how precious it is.* Memories of our devastating 4 a.m. phone call informing us of Jenny's death only six months earlier crept into my consciousness. I secretly struggled to repel the thoughts...to spare Jana the pain of watching me grieve...to avoid triggering the pain of her own memories...and to preserve this brief moment of serenity laced with mounting expectation.

Protect her by dealing silently with the despair that rips at your own heart, I ordered myself.

My self-talk was evidence of the twisted sidestep we had each unknowingly learned in our dance with grief—suppress our individual pain and sorrow to avoid triggering similar memories in the other person. And even more distance had grown between us through this tango of isolation that we'd begun to dance.

We knew we should reconnect. We *wanted* to reconnect. But even though our shoulders physically touched, an emotional chasm separated us. Stress and conflict during Jenny's years of rebellion had carved a canyon between us; torrents of grief following her death had widened its walls. During this first day on the Island we'd spent precious hours together in a tropical paradise. Our souls yearned to rediscover true intimacy, but our personal struggles with grief and our failed attempts to express our genuine emotions kept us at arm's distance.

Jana leaned forward in anticipation as she surveyed the setting sun. Other beach lovers had gathered up and down the shoreline. They looked expectantly toward the horizon, presumably to view the event we'd come to see.

The locals on the Big Island spoke of an amazing phenomenon—a green flash that occasionally lit the island's western shores as the last sliver of sun dipped below the distant horizon. Reportedly, the flash occurred precisely at sunset and momentarily transformed the ocean surface and sunset sky into a dazzling green. Their stories seemed dubious. The "Green Flash" sounded more like a comic book character than a real event. Still, we decided to check it out.

Distant clouds exploded in red and violet hues with a rich intensity that tainted even the white shorebirds.

"It's breathtaking, isn't it?" Jana whispered in awe.

"It *is* gorgeous." I struggled to reply and focused on the horizon through tear-filled eyes. Jana instantly perceived my pain.

"Are you okay?" she asked softly.

I languished in throbbing sorrow and a huge burden of guilt. "It just kills me sitting here on this beach without her. This was Jenny's dream destination, the place she begged us for years to visit 'on our next vacation,' and we just never made it happen. And now we finally visit the Big Island and bring her with us—her ashes."

"She would have loved to see this. And you know that she would have asked to have her ashes scattered here," Jana replied, as she danced the tango and carefully concealed her own emotions.

The sun touched the watery horizon.

Slowly, very slowly, the orange orb sunk into the ocean. Voices along the beach softened in a strangely reverent anticipation.

One-half submerged.

Three-quarters.

A thumbnail of light remained. This was the moment. Would we see it? And then... nothing.

No flash. No blinding light. Only disappointment. Distant clouds had obscured the final sun rays and prevented the green flash. We gathered our belongings.

"We still have seven more evenings—I'll bet we see it. Let's try again tomorrow night," Jana offered encouragingly, as we returned to our rented condo.

"I'd just like to know if it really happens. But the blazing sunset colors alone are worth another visit." It was, indeed, a welcome distraction, because I'd both yearned for, and dreaded, this trip for months.

For me this was a week of stress—financial stress for us to take such a vacation after losing our life savings—and it was a week of dread. We'd come to scatter Jenny's ashes.

The next evening we returned to the beach. Our dear friends, Mark and Karen, joined us. They had encouraged this December getaway because they knew how desperately our sunlight-starved Alaskan souls and broken hearts needed this 80-degree tropical therapy. They'd walked alongside us these last five years and had witnessed the crushing battles with our rebellious teen. They'd wept with us over the news of Jenny's death. After the funeral they'd watched us die in agonizing increments, as grief led us across the dance floor of despair and slowly tightened its fingers around our throats to strangle the very life from us.

On numerous occasions God had used Mark and Karen as resuscitators to breathe life back into us. They sat beside us now, praying for God Himself to breathe life into our grief-stricken souls.

The four of us searched the horizon. A partially drawn curtain of violet-tinged clouds awed our emotions—and yet stole the flash we hoped to see.

Evening three arrived. Once again, sunbeams of majestic splendor ignited a firestorm of colors in the distant clouds—the same clouds that later extinguished the mystical flash we yearned to witness.

Evening four... evening five... evening six. And each evening a dichotomy of emotions that pivoted between awe and frustration.

Evening seven arrived. Tomorrow we'd depart for Anchorage. If such a thing as the green flash existed, this would be our last chance to see it.

"Do you think this will be the night? If not, we just may have to come back to Hawaii and try again!" Jana's optimism was contagious.

"Hope so, but either way I'm eager to return to the Islands!"

My dread had passed. The week had challenged us, but God provided many signs of His presence. And the day before, we'd accomplished our goal of scattering Jenny's ashes in a secluded ocean cove near towering rocks. But something else happened amidst that agonizing event—something changed. A mysterious, emotional shift occurred within each of us during our private memorial... a change we couldn't quite define. Before, we lived and grieved independently, "protecting" each other through withdrawal while slowing dying in isolation. Afterward, we felt each other's presence—a spark of unity had ignited between us and opened a doorway of connection.

For the first time in months, maybe years, we'd labored *together* to reach the secret destination where we'd released Jenny's ashes. We'd openly ached *together,* as we'd solemnly remembered her life and then emotionally let her go. And we'd triumphed *together* in the completion of this heart-wrenching task. The searing pain of grief was still very real, and very near, but we had broken through an invisible barrier. We'd deliberately taken the first steps into the chasm toward one another as husband and wife.

We squinted at the blazing ocean surface to view this final sunset.

No distant clouds...a good sign...but then, we'd been disappointed before.

The sun touched the ocean and began its slow decent.

Halfway.

Three-quarters. Still, no clouds. Nervous anticipation tightened our stomachs. Another minute passed.

Could this be the day?

The final sliver met the horizon.

Kazaap!

For a split second the ocean, the western sky, and the thread of remaining sun blazed a brilliant green, bathing us in a rich, emerald glow.

"The green flash!...Did you see it?...It's real!" Jana shouted. The four of us jumped up and celebrated with joy over the rare beauty our eyes had embraced.

Muffled "Oooohhs" and "Aaaahhhs" drifted up and down the beach. Some clapped. Others stared in awe, as they tried to comprehend what had just happened. It had passed so quickly, like a trick of the eyes, but it had been no trick.

It had been a miracle—the phenomenon, the timing, and the significance.

From a scientific point of view, the flash is an optical event that occurs under perfect meteorological conditions in which the clear ocean water becomes a liquid prism for the final beams of sunlight. The green rays of the spectrum pass through the shallow water and produce a brief, but beautiful, emerald flash.

From a philosophical view, *the flash is the moment of change*, an emerald beacon that signals the knife-edge boundary between day and night. One minute, sunlight. Then, *kazaap!* It's night.

For us, the green flash included these aspects and much more—it represented a *spiritual* breakthrough in which God confirmed, through this dazzling miracle, that He had orchestrated this week and this moment to breathe life into our dying souls and our languishing marriage. It was another shared experience, an *awe* experience that confirmed the change between us.

Before the *kazaap!*—in fact, just the day before—we had sensed each other's emotional need to reconnect. After the *kazaap!,* we knew God was with us *as a couple* and hope began to flow. Before our Hawaii trip, we'd thrashed in a sea of despair among giant, crashing waves of grief, separate and alone. But then, the flash, and *kazaap!*—we began moving toward one another. Waves of grief still pummeled us after we left the Island, but from this week onward we would stay afloat and ride their crests *together* as God began the long process of rebuilding our marriage.

The green flash.

It's real. It's quick. It marks the moment of change. In an instant, something that was one way suddenly becomes something different. And it often triggers a process of further transformation.

The Bible talks about two different kinds of spiritual transformation—*instantaneous transformation,* like the green flash, *and incremental transformation,* which is change that happens over a period of time. In this chapter I'll discuss instantaneous change, the *kazaaps!* in our lives, while Jana will discuss incremental change in the next chapter.

A *kazaap!* also occurs in the gem-cutting process I follow as a lapidary. It, too, marks a fascinating change between darkness and light.

THE FIRST CUT—
A GEMSTONE REVEALED

Let's quickly review where we are in the cutting of this ametrine that sits on my lapidary desk. I've examined this stone thoroughly. I know it intimately. I've peered deeply within its core to identify every fracture, inclusion, and defect. I know its strongest color orientation—the position that best displays its unique beauty. From these details I've chosen a design—one that will vividly reflect the dazzling purple and yellow, bicolor brilliance of this stone. I mount and secure a coarse grinding lap on the motor spindle that protrudes through the top surface of the lapidary machine. The lap is a flat metal disk that spins at moderate speed. Coarse diamond grit, an incredibly hard abrasive, embeds the lap's upper surface. I set the exact angle on the machine's cutting head, attach the dop with the stone, and turn on the motor. A soft *hummm* fills the room.

Now comes the moment for which I've labored.

This is what it's all about—the first cut.

With only a few brief slashes on the coarse lap, the stone will be transformed into its final design—almost instantly.

This action can frighten an apprentice lapidary. It's unnerving to press a small piece of rough valued at several hundred dollars against a coarse, spinning grinding wheel. But with experience comes confidence. Already I imagine this gem in its final state of glory, and I do not hesitate.

Slowly, gently, I lower the stone onto the spinning lap.

A rough, gritty *whirrrr* resonates at the touch.

Particles fly through the air. I hear and feel the raspy lap as it cuts fast and deep, ripping through the rough's marred surface. These first cuts require a very light touch to avoid overcutting. With only slight pressure the lap grinds away the stone's deep internal flaws.

The first facet is complete.

I rotate the dop and stone a precise number of degrees, cut another surface, and continue the process. The design takes shape. Friction creates heat, which can damage the gem and soften the wax joint that secures the stone to the dop, causing it to shift. To avoid this I apply water to the lap with a saturated brush to cool the stone and sweep away the residue.

Whirrr, whirr, whirr.

The water I've applied saturates the stone's rough-cut surface.

Kazaap! An amber flash bursts forth from inside the stone.

This initial flash of light marks a moment of radical transformation. For the first time the color and clarity hidden within the stone are released. Why? Cutting away the flawed areas enabled the external light to enter the stone and bounce back unhindered. *Light must shine in before it reflects out.*

The first flash is an exhilarating experience. It confirms the design I've chosen, and it reflects the nature of the stone itself. An intense flash in the early stages of a roughly cut stone speaks of its clarity and the intensity of its color. Cutting a stone is almost a spiritual experience for me. The analogies of gemstone transformation closely parallel my own changed life.

MY KAZAAP!

As a teenager I was a "glowing stone" that cried out to God. I'd heard of Him...I didn't know Him. I knew of Jesus and even believed that He died on the cross for the sins of the world, but I'd never personalized His sacrifice nor sought Him specifically.

God heard my cry. He looked down from heaven, saw the glimmer in my heart—the desire to know Him—and lovingly picked me up. As He studied me, a plan formed in His mind: He would introduce me to a new type of teaching, a fresh paradigm in which to see His Son Jesus, and ultimately a series of "cuts" would remove my own birthmarks and blemishes so that I could reflect the light of Christ.

God led me to a new type of Bible study—one that focused exclusively upon His Son.[1] Hungrily, I consumed what the Bible said about Jesus. He *was* the Son of God. He died to pay the penalty for *my* sin. If I would confess His name and believe in what He did for me, personally, I would be a son of God. I would have eternal life.

Over that three-month study, I said "yes" to Jesus multiple times and accepted that He died for *my* sins upon the cross. I invited His bright light to penetrate my dark heart. *Kazaap!*

I was changed, just like the first cut of a stone. Before, I knew of God but had no relationship; now He was my Abba (Daddy), my Father. Before, I was filled with darkness. Now Light penetrated and filled my heart. One moment my spirit was dead, the next moment my spirit was alive. My heart bore witness to the truth in 2 Corinthians 5:17: "Therefore if anyone is in Christ, he is a new creature; the old things passed away; behold, new things have come."

The change in my heart required that my sin be cut away; spiritual light cannot enter nor be released if the blackness of sin blocks it.

The "cut" has always been a "big deal" to God—it's the confirmation of our covenant with Him, and it's a concept worth exploring. Let's consider what it means when God initiates the "cut" that brings us into covenant with Him.

A CONTRAST OF TWO CUTS: THE PHYSICAL AND SPIRITUAL

Sonograms were rare almost thirty years ago when we started our family. You learned the sex of your baby at birth and not before. I suspected that our firstborn child would be a boy. For generations, the firstborn child in the Chatham family had been male. *Wrong*! Julie came screaming and laughing into our world, full of softness and smiles.

I had no doubt that our second child would be a boy. Surely statistics would triumph, right? But after ten hours of labor the doctor proclaimed, "You have a girl." In shock, I actually asked the doctor, "Are you sure?" He held Jenny up, naked and kicking, and with a hint of irritation replied, "You look and decide."

The doctor's announcement surprised me, but I love my daughters. I can't imagine fatherhood otherwise. And we were spared the decision faced by many parents of male children of whether or not to perform a procedure called "circumcision."

In Old Testament times Jewish parents of a newborn son faced no such decision: They had no choice. The Law required circumcision—a painful procedure in which the foreskin of a baby boy's penis was cut away on the eighth day after birth.

Why would God require the "cutting away" of flesh? Because circumcision was a sign of something very significant. God said, "And you shall be circumcised in the flesh of your foreskin, and it shall be the sign of the covenant between Me and you."[2]

A covenant is an agreement in which two parties commit to certain obligations. God made a covenant with Abraham, the father of the Jewish nation, and, as His part of the covenant, He promised to protect, care for, and love Abraham and his descendants forever. In return, Abraham and his generations were to honor, obey, and trust the Lord.[3] The covenant carried with it the idea of belonging—God said, "I will walk among you and be Your God, and you will be my people."[4]

Circumcision was the sign that the Jews belonged to God. God kept His end of the bargain, but Abraham's descendants (the Jews) frequently strayed and ignored their end. As a result, God would design a new covenant, a better covenant that would include both Jew and Gentile. And He would choose a different sign for the covenant because circumcision had a weakness—*it altered the flesh but left the spirit untouched.*[5]

In my younger years I witnessed firsthand a mark that also carried with it this weakness.

THE WEAKNESS OF THE PHYSICAL CUT

As a young man, roundup at the Chatham ranch was the biggest event of the year. We Texans saddled our horses before dawn and rode through dew-covered grass and sleepy woods to round up the cattle and "drive" them to an awaiting pen. Unlike the movies of the early West, we didn't rope and throw each animal. We drove the cattle single file through a chute—two long, narrow, wooden fences only four feet apart that ran side by side. At the end was a metal squeeze chute with two moveable walls made of steel bars, which firmly secured each animal so we could administer shots and perform other unpleasant tasks.

I learned about branding at the squeeze chute.

Several steel rods with a "C" symbol at the end lay heating in a propane-fired oven. Just before releasing the animal from the chute, my uncle firmly pressed the red-hot branding iron against the animal's hip for about three seconds.

Hiss! White smoke and the pungent smell of burning hair and flesh filled my nostrils. The animal bolted from the opened chute sporting a fresh "C" brand.

Kazaap! In an instant the animal changed from being an unclaimed, free-roving steer to a possession of the Chatham ranch.

The "C" brand that marked each animal's hide guaranteed protection, food, and care if ill, yet I never met a steer that desired an intimate relationship with its owner. Neither did possession impart loyalty. If the fence was down and the grass looked greener, the critter immediately abandoned its home in pursuit of better pastures.

In a similar way, the physical cut of circumcision marked the Jewish nation as God's people but could never promote the intimate relationship He desired. Their hearts were hard. God's prophet, Zechariah, described man's depraved heart as flint—a tough, hard, and opaque rock.[6] Moses and other prophets continually admonished the Jews to "circumcise your heart... stiffen your neck no longer," but they refused to listen.[7] God's "chosen people" selfishly strayed to other forbidden pastures and worshipped the idols of man rather than their Creator.

Man's heart of flint required transformation. Ezekiel prophesied of a future change: "I shall take the heart of stone out of their flesh and give them a heart of flesh, that they may walk in My statutes... and do them."[8]

All along, God had a better plan, a superior covenant in mind for mankind. He knew that circumcision could no more change man's heart than a "C" on the hip could induce loyalty from a maverick steer. Intimacy required internal change; it required that the power of sin be broken. Hebrews 10:16 and 17 (NLT) speaks of the second covenant:

> This is the covenant I will make with them after that time, says the Lord. I will put my laws in their hearts and I will write them on their minds... their sins and lawless acts I will remember no more.

Unlike the previous covenant, this new covenant would deal with the sin issue once and for all. And through this covenant, God's people would know His Law by instinct—what's right and wrong—as if it were written on their hearts.

How could this be?

First, it would require the death of God's Son, Jesus Christ: "Christ is the mediator of a new covenant, that those who are called may receive the promised eternal inheritance—now that he has died as a ransom to set them free from the sins committed under the first covenant."[9]

AN EMERALD, A GREEN FLASH, AND A CHANGED LIFE

When we accept Christ as Savior, His blood rips through the marred corruption that darkens our heart, breaks our bondage from sin, and *kazaap!*—the Green Flash—Christ's light illuminates our heart. In gemstone terminology it's akin to the green flash of light from the first deep cut of a precious emerald.

Emeralds have been sought and treasured by mankind since at least the early days of Egypt (approximately 3500 B.C.). Cleopatra's passion for emeralds is well-documented. Emeralds are extremely valued. For example, a fine diamond can sell for tens of thousands of dollars per carat, but Elizabeth Taylor's fine emerald brooch sold for a record $280,000 per carat.[10]

Emeralds occur worldwide, though very few localities produce the large, deep-green gems. Today's high quality stones are produced primarily from mines in Columbia, South America. The Chivor mine was first discovered and worked by the Aztec Indians until invaded and conquered by the Spanish in 1537.[11]

Most natural emeralds are heavily clouded with inclusions and fractures. Man-made emeralds are dark green and clear. Inclusions validate the stone as natural. It's no wonder that a large, deep-green, and near-flawless natural emerald is unfathomably valuable.

An emerald is the candidate gemstone to represent Jesus Christ. Scripture suggests that the emerald represents Christ through its association with a heavenly priesthood.

The emerald was the fourth stone in the breastpiece of the priestly ephod and the fourth foundation stone of the "heavenly Jerusalem," as envisioned by the Apostle John (Exodus 28:6-12; Revelation 21:10-20). In Scripture, the "fourth" occurrence symbolizes the Tribe of Judah, from which Jesus' lineage through Mary and David descended.

In a vision of heaven, John describes the throne of God as being surrounded by a rainbow of emerald. The rainbow is God's symbol of His peace covenant with mankind.[12] John's vision links the rainbow—God's symbol of peace, with the emerald as Christ—God's instrument of peace who is called "the Prince of Peace."

But what could change the hearts of God's people so they would know His Law by instinct? That question involves a "Who," rather than a "what."

THE POWER OF THE SPIRITUAL CUT

We've all changed a burnt-out light bulb. What do we do the moment it's replaced? We flip on the switch! The new bulb only "glows" once the power flows through it.

The moment Christ's blood frees us from the dark bondage of sin, our hearts are "cut" by the power of the Holy Spirit. *The very Spirit of God comes to dwell inside us.* To use the light bulb metaphor, we become a "new bulb" and then, *kazaap!* the Holy Spirit cuts into our being and a switch is flipped. We glow with a new power—not our power but God's power that is at work within us. This heavenly infusion in earthly followers is not a new thing; it's been happening for centuries.

Jesus told the apostles after His resurrection that they were not to leave Jerusalem but to "wait for... the Holy Spirit... you will receive power when the Holy Spirit comes upon you."[13]

Why?

The apostles' future ministry and their spiritual lives in Christ could only be sustained through the power of the Holy Spirit. That same Spirit is given to us today. "The Holy Spirit has been sent by the Father to assist you in all the practical matters of Christian living. He is your number one Helper."[14] What does God's "help" look like?

- His power gives you strength to choose who you will obey—God or your fleshy desires.[15]
- The Holy Spirit gives you gifts to help others—gifts such as knowledge, wisdom, teaching, evangelism, and healing.[16]
- The Spirit teaches you and comforts you.
- The Spirit convicts you of sin.
- The Spirit warns you of temptations and helps you overcome them.
- The Spirit guides you into all truth.[17]

A pastor in our church frequently shares this statement about the Holy Spirit, "You just know in your 'knower' that the Spirit is living within you. He helps you in those situations where you can't help yourself."[18]

In summary, the "cut" of the old covenant was a physical cut that failed to change the heart. The "cut" of the new covenant is a spiritual cut which changes the heart. We are sealed by God's Spirit—the Spirit is the mark, our brand, our sign of ownership (Ephesians 1:13).

Let's take a look at one man whose life was drastically transformed by an encounter with Jesus and the Holy Spirit.

SAUL: GOD'S CHOSEN GEM

The year was about 34 A.D.[19] A spiritual light had dawned in Judea. Its early rays now penetrated the darkness of the surrounding nations, as Jesus desired to illuminate Gentile hearts throughout the Mediterranean region and eventually the world.

God needed a special messenger to accomplish this task. The Master Lapidary looked down on the streambed of humanity and saw a glimmer seen only by His eye. He picked up the living stone and examined the calloused, marred, surface. This stone possessed a radically zealous heart for God, a ferocious commitment to obedience, and a deep knowledge of the Old Law. This gem's name was Saul.

Saul was a Pharisee (Jewish religious sect) who believed that salvation and a relationship with God required near-perfect obedience to ancestral traditions and the Mosaic Law. Pharisees labored under rules of performance to "earn" salvation.

Some call me a fanatic…a "Hebrew of Hebrews"…and maybe I am. If only my brothers would join me, we could stamp out these heretics.[20] *Stoning was a fitting end to the one they called Stephen. I watched him die. I would have cast those stones myself if I'd been older—but I'm not holding their coats any longer! I will avenge Jerusalem of this false religion!*[21]

Deceived and foolish rebels. How could any true Hebrew elevate a "man" to the status of God? And how blind are these "Christians" who worship this man? After all, he died on a Roman cross before hundreds of witnesses. This rebellion must cease—and I intend to stop it!

A new heresy called "Christianity" had infiltrated the synagogues of Galilee and Judea. Violent resistance exploded as hardened Jewish leaders fought back.

None fought harder than Saul.

Finally, Damascus is in sight!

It's only noon, and with one more hour of travel ahead we still have time to present the documents to the local priest.

Yes! Finally, I can reach outside Judea and crush the heretical uprising beyond her borders. The local Damascus leadership would never interfere with the authorizations I hold in my hand—letters from the Jerusalem High Priest himself.

"Hurry on," Saul ordered his traveling companions. "We're almost there. Let's show the rebels in Damascus the consequences of worshiping this man they call 'Jesus.'"

And then... *Kazaap!* A flash of light bolted from heaven and struck Saul.

He fell to his knees on the road. A booming voice from heaven spoke with such authority that it made him tremble:

"Saul, Saul, why are you persecuting Me?"[22]

Dumbfounded and confused he voiced a simple question: "Who are You, Lord?"

The Lord replied, "*I am Jesus* whom you are persecuting" (emphasis ours).

Jesus? But you're dead. How is it that I hear your voice? I tortured every witness that insisted that you rose from the grave. I called them liars and slapped their faces. I denounced them as traitors to God and to Rome. I ordered them to be flogged and sent to prison. How can you speak to me? You're dead... I'm alive!

Saul lay humbled on the roadside, lower than the filthy gravel that buried his face. His tasseled robe and holy orders suddenly seemed insignificant in comparison to the revelation that perhaps he'd been wrong about the identity of Jesus.

The Lord continued, "...get up and enter the city and it will be told you *what you must do*" (emphasis ours).

Obediently, Saul pushed himself off the ground in an effort to stand, only to realize that he had another problem.

The brilliant, bright light that had cut through his soul moments earlier had blinded his eyes.

Saul could not see.

BLINDED BY THE LIGHT

The prominent and feared avenger of God entered Damascus led by the hand of his companions—broken, dirty, and blind. He spent the next three days without food, drink, or sight, waiting to hear "what he must do." He waited alone, in darkness, painfully aware that unfounded hatred and murderous error dominated his entire life.[23] And though his physical sight was gone, his spiritual eyes were wide open.

I slaughtered servants of the Most High. I tore apart families—slayed parents whose children will someday judge me. Even blinded, I still see their eyes.

I was a fool. I missed it. The Law speaks about the coming Messiah—His birth, life, death, and resurrection. It was all there, and I missed it.

Jesus was, no, IS *the Messiah—He lives. I blasphemed God. I murdered His servants. "What must I do?" What* can *I do? Why didn't He kill me on the roadside as I deserved?*

On the third day God sent Ananias to Saul's dark world to offer light. "Arise and be baptized," Ananias said, as he laid hands upon Saul.[24]

Kazaap! Saul confessed Jesus as his Lord. In an instant he was changed. The Holy Spirit entered Saul's heart. Immediately, he regained his physical sight, but his spiritual vision would be changed forever. He would never see the world, or himself, in the same way.

Saul became a minister and witness to the Gentiles and established churches for the very Lord he once persecuted. He understood the significance of God's covenant and the spiritual marks of possession. He personally acknowledged them later in life: "From now on let no one cause trouble for me, for I bear on my body the brand-marks of Jesus."[25]

If one who was so bent on destroying Jesus could change and become His most devoted follower, can we do no less? You may think, *Yeah, Saul could make such a change because he was chosen to* be an apostle. I'm certainly no apostle; why would Jesus ever change me? The answer to that question is this: Because Jesus loves you and me as much as He does Saul, *and* because if Jesus can change me (Jim), he can certainly change you!

JIM'S RELEASE FROM BONDAGE

I shared how the *kazaap!* of Christ severed the bonds of sin that corrupted my heart. Now I'll share how the power of the Holy Spirit helped me conquer impure sexual thoughts.

In an earlier chapter I shared how exposure to pornography at an early age had a grip on my life. Like many hormone-fueled teenagers, I struggled with flashbacks of images and lustful passions—if you're a male, you know what I mean.

After graduation, we moved to Dallas for my first job in an oil industry research facility. A popular television series, *Dallas*, had captivated the nation and had set new fashion trends for women that made provocative dress acceptable, even in the boardroom. The research lab was a competitive environment for us technical types *and* for the administrative gals intent on climbing the executive ladder. Big hair, short skirts, and low necklines were standard attire for the business-professional Texas woman. Those in the lab were scantily clad and *real* friendly. The setting provided high-octane, sensual fuel for a burning imagination.

One female assistant just around the corner from my office could have been a stand-in for Victoria Principal on the *Dallas* series. Dark, lustful thoughts bombarded me each time we passed in the hall. I struggled to resist but usually failed—until I accepted Christ as my personal Savior, and, *kazaap!* a new resolve rose within me to keep my mind pure.

It was another warm afternoon in the lab. The white walls and ceiling gave the long hallways a sterile, almost clinical appearance. Blinding sunlight poured through the evenly spaced, ceiling-height glass windows. Suddenly, there she was—"dolled up," pulsing with color and life. She brushed by and smiled.

The familiar lustful imaginings rose in me, but this time I appealed for God's powerful intervention, "Lord, help me. Take these thoughts away!" Suddenly the images vanished, and they didn't return. I clearly remember a peculiar mental "blankness" that simply snuffed out the images. It was the first day of relief from a plague of mental sexual bondage. And the relief persists to this day.

YOUR KAZAAP!

When it comes to Jesus, have you experienced a *kazaap!*

There must be a flash—a time you can point to when He became real and personal for you. Many believers can name the week, day, or minute that the Lord changed their heart and they knew they were different.

Others, like me, can't identify the precise moment of their acceptance of Jesus but can point to specific moments of revelation when they entered into a new level of intimacy with Christ.

When it comes to the Holy Spirit, have you experienced a *kazaap!* Have you had moments in which a holy power surged through you, or you were suddenly filled with wisdom and strength that were not your own? Have new talents emerged in your life—a supernatural ability to teach, heal, or serve in some way?

If you haven't received a *kazaap!* pray and ask God to send His Spirit to teach and reveal Jesus to you personally. Pray for those specific spiritual gifts that you sense a strange yearning to possess. Ask Him to open your eyes to the needs of those around you and to flood you with His presence and His power to interact. Pray for His specific intervention to open doors to those works you were created specifically to fulfill.

As you pray, check your heart. Are you looking for the Spirit to work? Are you surrendered to God's Spirit in your life? "The

Spirit-filled life begins once we are absolutely and thoroughly convinced that we can do nothing apart from the indwelling strength of the Holy Spirit."[26]

If you are trying to do life on your own, stop! Depend utterly upon Him and, *kazaap!* you will be changed.

2 GEMS

PRAYER:

Dear Lord, thank You for giving me Your Holy Spirit. The Holy Spirit is my Helper, my Comforter, my Teacher—the One who gives me strength and wisdom. Holy Spirit, fill me. Saturate me with Your presence and Your power. Release in me new spiritual gifts that I may honor my heavenly Father and help others. Amen

---

God can change me in an instant *(kazaap!)*.

- When we believe in Jesus, God sends His Spirit to dwell inside us.

- The Holy Spirit directs us and helps us follow God's ways.

- Apart from God's Spirit, we can do nothing.

- In the power of God's Spirit, we can do all things.

CHAPTER 7

The Daily Grind

" **T**HERE IS AN eagle in me that wants to soar, and there is a hippopotamus in me that wants to wallow in the mud." I (Jana) relate strongly to this quote by Cal Sandburg, do you?

Take a moment and reflect upon a time when you enjoyed a mountaintop experience, the sensation of soaring high like an eagle. Perhaps when you received kudos from someone you admired or the successful completion of a dreaded task. Or maybe you enjoyed a vacation so spectacular that it blotted out all the cares of the world. The memory brings a smile to your face, right? Who doesn't desire a carefree, *on top of the world* feeling?

Now think back to a time when you found yourself miserable, wallowing through the mud like the hippopotamus in Sandburg's quote. Fingers grimy as you clawed through the muck of a horrendous fight with someone you love. Bloody knees as you groped through the shattered shards of self-respect after being dismissed from your job. Not a fun memory, is it?

Nearly everyone I know craves a relatively calm life, accompanied by *occasional* mountaintop experiences, while avoiding, at all costs, any form of valley-crawling.

Not me. The majority of my life I sought to live in a constant state of soaring or wallowing—the mountaintop or the valley seemed to

ADRENALINE JUNKIE SELF-TEST

Take this self-test to help you identify if you might be over-adrenalized.

1. Are you often in a hurry, rushing from one thing to the next?
2. During a typical day, do you work with intensity on something that seems urgent?
3. Do you tend to do two or three things at once to be more efficient?
4. Are you productive, busy, or active almost all the time?
5. Do you regularly rely on caffeine to feel energetic and focused?
6. If you're not working on something, do you rely on stimulation from activity, entertainment, or noise?
7. When you're resting, do you feel fidgety, pace, drum your fingers, tap your feet, or chew fast?
8. If you're idle, do you feel guilty or restless?
9. When you're waiting, are you usually uncomfortably impatient (e.g., looking at your watch, getting upset, or counting items in the short-order line)?
10. When you go to bed at night, do you typically think about all the things that you didn't get done and need to get done?
11. When you go on vacation, do you feel empty, bored, or depressed?
12. Do you often have physical stress symptoms like gastric distress, rapid heartbeat, headaches, muscle pain, teeth grinding at night, and sleep problems?

Scoring: "Yes" answers to four or more items indicate that you may be depending on adrenaline and related hormones like cortisol to manage daily stresses. For diagnoses and treatment consult in person with a doctor or psychotherapist.[1]

make no difference because both produced a chemical in my body that I desperately needed: adrenaline.

I am a recovering adrenaline junkie.

My addiction began at an early age, as a result of my desperate fight to survive. When my mother held me against the gas bathroom heater and I was severely burned, when my brother tied me to a clothes line pole and forgot about me for hours, or when I stepped between my cousin and her husband who was attacking her with a knife, adrenaline pulsed through my tiny body and gave me the will to press through the traumatic events. My safety was threatened so often that, by age twelve, I'd developed a keen sensitivity to danger. Whenever the light in my brain flashed danger, adrenaline surged through my body and caused my heart to beat wildly. The constant release of fight-or-flight chemicals changed my body's ability to process and eliminate the drugs. The more stress/chaos/trauma my body experienced, the more pleasure-giving endorphins were required to maintain homeostasis. Over the years I required more and more adrenaline to achieve the same pleasure-giving endorphins.[2]

As a young adult I lived in a constant state of adrenaline rushes. The continuous high levels of adrenaline impaired my ability to processes emotions in a healthy manner.[3] In my thirties I didn't realize that I was addicted to adrenaline, nor did I realize that I unknowingly created situations to keep my adrenal levels elevated. Some people live life in the fast lane; I lived life in the *oncoming-traffic lane*. Whether a mountaintop experience, a dark valley, or a life filled with busyness, all produced stress, which caused my adrenal glands to pump out adrenaline, which gave me the "rush" to which I'd become addicted.[4]

Our culture esteems busyness. To be important you have to be busy. That philosophy suited me because I erroneously believed I was more important when I was busy, and busyness produced stress, which caused my adrenal glands to kick into high gear.

"Let's get together," a friend offered. She stepped in front of me, as I raced down the hall to my next appointment.

"I'd love to," I said. Quickly I flipped open my Day-Timer®, which recorded my appointments, and scanned the white squares for an open date.

She gasped. Then she reached over and flipped the pages of my Day-Timer®. Her disapproving glare transferred from the notes on the pages to me. The look on her face made me feel like I was looking squarely into my mother's judgmental, condemning eyes. I went from feeling like a confident woman on top of her game to feeling like an insecure little girl who couldn't do anything right.

"Jana, what are you doing?" In a tone mixed with disgust and dismay, she closed my calendar and said, while shaking her head, "Look at yourself. When you get your life under control we'll meet." Then she turned and walked away.

At this moment, I had a choice. I could embrace her rebuff as a moment of teaching, a moment to reevaluate the frenzy of my life and remove unnecessary activity. Did I do that? No. Instead I stuffed the issue of my busyness and purchased a new planner in which I recorded my schedule in abbreviated code with small letters so I didn't appear overly busy. I didn't change my life, only how others might perceive my life.

Then Jenny died—something that is never on a mother's schedule. Immediately a flurry of activity and emotion pushed the needle on my adrenaline meter to a level beyond "high." We flew from Alaska to Texas, organized the memorial, made decisions about her cremation, cleaned out her apartment, then flew back home. Two weeks later I flew to Washington State where I was the matron of honor in a wedding and responsible for baking the wedding cake. The day after the wedding I drove to Montana to visit loved ones who had moved overseas—all of this activity while I hobbled around on crutches.

This was insane!

Internally, I felt as if all of life should stop because Jenny had died, but externally I raced through these important life events at breakneck speed with a broken ankle and a broken heart. After several months of nonstop adrenaline rushes, my life came to a screeching halt. All activity stopped. I tumbled down, down, down into a deep valley of grief in which I could hardly crawl out of bed. If someone had asked me to paint a picture that represented my life during the two years before and after Jenny's death I'd have painted a series of jagged mountaintops whose gloomy shadows cast darkness upon deep gorges below. I could not continue to live in this state of extremism. Something had to change. I made a conscious decision that it was time to redo my personal landscape; it was time to paint peaceful, smooth meadows and quiet reflective ponds.

I needed a different type of life—a life of steadiness and peace where I could *be still and know God*. But even in this stillness I knew there could be times of mountaintop experiences. I could still have excitement—an excitement fueled by God, *not* by things, people, stressful chaos or circumstances of my own making. My goal was to stop my internal motor from racing but not to the point that it idled or died. I wanted to move through life at a steady pace and enjoy the journey.

I needed a getaway—a place of solitude and peace where I could physically *do nothing* and *be still*, which hopefully would encourage my spirit to settle down and relax. I needed a place where I didn't feel emotional triggers connected with Jenny's death looming around every corner.

Jim and I planned a trip to the Oregon coast during the off-season with two specific goals: first, to have an uninterrupted and quiet week to process Jenny's death, individually and as a couple; second, for me to figure out how to implement changes in my life.

WALK WITH ME

Seven days of peace.

Seven days of endless quiet hours to reconnect as a couple.

Seven days to leisurely walk the beach together and alone.

Seven days to quiet my body, soul, and spirit... to become still, to talk and listen to God.

On the first evening I unpacked my suitcase at our beachside condo, with great expectancy of listening to the grand cadence of the ocean waves as they splashed against the sandy shore. I yearned to breathe in the clean, fresh salt air and feel the warm sand encase my toes. I looked forward to becoming enmeshed in the magnificent beach ambiance to help turn off my revved-up, internal motor. Admittedly I still sought a "high," but not the highs of my past, which might have included seeing new sites or engaging in an adrenaline-rush adventure. No, I wanted a God-high—a spiritual mountaintop experience to fill the constant grieving abyss in my heart. I longed to hear His voice stir my soul, to feel my Lord's presence. I envisioned holy serenity enmeshed with the euphoria of hearing God's voice. *Did it even exist?*

The first morning I dashed to the beach, yearning to be with God and to hear from Him. The squeak of the squishy sand under my feet accompanied my anticipation. I scanned the horizon, acutely aware of God's grandeur and my own smallness. I sensed God's presence. He was close; He was above me and even around me yet beyond my reach. *Why couldn't I touch Him?*

Admittedly, following Jenny's death, I'd built a hard covering around my heart to keep other people from penetrating my vulnerable grief—a shell like the ones scattered along the beach. This shell protected my emotions, but had it also created a barrier between myself and God? I hated feeling separate from Him, and I prayed that He'd pull me close, crack my shell, and lift my spirit and emotions to His mountaintop.

I asked, like an excited child eagerly waiting on a surprise, *Today, God? Is it today? Will You draw me close, whisper to my heart, and pull me to Your mountaintop today?* My question hung in the heavy salt air with no response from God.

I turned around and retraced my footsteps back to the condo. Exhaling deeply, I said out loud, "Maybe tomorrow. Will You meet with me tomorrow, God?"

Six days I walked the beach morning, noon, and night and begged God to pull me close; each day I returned with the feeling that God was nearby but I couldn't reach Him. On our last morning my optimistic nature took over, and I popped out of bed for my walk...eager...anticipating a spirit-lifting encounter with God. Low tide exposed small crabs—a banquet breakfast for the shore birds. I collected some shells along with my thoughts.

I picked up a stick and scribbled the letters J-E-N-N-Y in the wet sand canvas. A foamy wave covered my feet with bitter cold fingers of salt water. I reached towards Jenny's name, trying to protect it from being pulled into the ocean. A flood of memories washed over me. Our two blonde-haired little girls in a different time on a different beach, giggling, chasing sea gulls and building sand castles that were washed away by the tide. Then another memory, another beach, another time. Mexico, our last family vacation when the girls were teenagers. Each wave that washed upon the shore caused another memory to wash over me. *God, so much washes away every passing year. So many memories, good and bad, come and go like the crest of each wave.*

I stood, walked to a dryer spot and plopped down onto the sand. Sigh.

God, I know You are here with me as I relive these memories. Please, please, talk to me. Please let me hear You. Please shatter the hard shell around my heart. The roar of the surf drowned out my moans. The harder I tried to listen to God the louder the surf became. God's silence was deafening. An overwhelming emptiness swallowed me. *Why can't I hear You speak to my spirit? Please, just a single word or a simple vision.*

I picked up a handful of sand and allowed it to flow through my fingers like an hourglass counting down time. All week I'd walked the beach filled with anticipation of an encounter with God, only to be met with disappointment.

Okay, God, I showed up every day. I sought You every day. Where are You?

I crammed my heels into the sand and squirmed to settle deeper into the soft, dry beach. Frustrated, I thrust my hands deep into the warm sand, grabbed two fistfuls and threw them in the air. I was mad. Mad at myself for having childish expectations that God would show up. Mad for thinking that God was different than my earthly father who'd disappointed me all my life. My stomach churned, just like when I was in grade school, as I sat on the porch step for hours waiting for my father to pick me up for the weekend. He never showed. I felt abandoned, rejected, and unloved. The days this week were like those hours of waiting to be adored by a dad who never came, never loved and really never wanted me.

I grabbed another fistful of sand and threw it to the ground.

No matter what I did as a child I couldn't make my father love me, so why would I expect God to love me? As soon as the thought entered my mind I argued myself out of it. *No! God is not like my father. He* does *love me. He* does*!*

I jumped up and brushed the sand off my backside, desperately trying to brush away my conflicting emotions as easily as the sand. I looked over my shoulder and realized my walk had taken me a long way down the beach. *Better head back.*

I turned around. The walk down the beach had been a journey through memories in my past, losses and wounds that weighed heavily on my heart. The walk back to the condo meant facing the reality of my present—the reality of Jim and I enduring another year without our beloved daughter. Painful emotions pressed upon me at every turn—in my waking and sleeping, in my going to and coming from, in my past and present. I was so tired of painful emotions and feeling like I was being held down by something heavy. I stopped and brushed myself off again to symbolically rid myself of the weighty feelings.

I forced myself to focus on good things, happy thoughts. Even though God wasn't meeting me here on the beach in the way I wanted, I had seen evidence of Him working between Jim and me these past few days. *God, I am grateful that Jim and I used this past week to open up and process painful frustrations.* After Jenny's death Jim and I had become experts in our own sidestep dance to protect the other while we separately floundered in emotional anguish. This week, we'd synchronized our steps and plunged beyond superficial discussions about the years of Jenny's rebellion leading up to her death. We'd shared our perspectives and the reasons behind the actions which had led to our parental polarization. We'd shared honestly, but respectfully, making it a point to be gentle rather than critical with one another.

Thank you, Lord, for providing this place and time for us to tenderly listen to one another and not to judge each other. Our quiet and relaxing vacation had morphed into gut-wrenching conversations as we'd relived a series of painful memories—the first 4 a.m. police call, Jenny's first DUI, her drug usage, and her eating disorder. We'd each shared our justifying reasons for why we'd behaved as we had. For the first time I understood why Jim had taken certain actions, and he realized why I'd responded as I had. This new insight slowly rebuilt intimacy in our marriage. We knew strengthening our marriage was not a quick fix, but we were obviously moving forward in healing.

Yes, Lord, it has been good to share our individual pain and grief with one another. Suddenly I stopped dead in my tracks.

Is this it, God? Is this my mountaintop experience—not a euphoric encounter with You but healing in my marriage? I had removed my protective shell with Jim. Finally I could feel again, but it wasn't the kind of emotion I wanted. I wanted to feel joy and passion again, to be filled up with You, not to be drained by raw emotions of painful memories. I let out a heavy sigh, reached down, and picked up a broken sand dollar.

I lifted my head and gazed across the horizon.

Then slowly, *very* slowly, God spoke... with a very quiet voice to my heart.

Walk... with... Me.

What? Walk with You?

I threw my hands up in the air and screamed out loud. "Arrrrgggg!" Several startled gulls quickly burst into flight. Irritated, I snapped, "What do You think I've been doing, God? I've been walking all week."

Softy He spoke again.

Walk with Me.

What are You trying to tell me? I don't understand.

In the distance several boys enthusiastically played soccer, a black Lab attacked the white waves in search of his tennis ball, and a photographer set up his tripod to capture the sunset. Shore birds scampered quickly across the sand in front of me. It seemed everything around me was carefree and happy-go-lucky.

I gazed upon the vast blue ocean and surveyed the flat horizon. Before me a spectacular sky and an expansive beach. No mountains to climb. No valleys to crawl through. No adrenalin-producing challenges. I was alone... *with Him*. I bowed my head and heard His soft voice deep within my spirit speak once more.

Walk with Me.

God, I'm exhausted and totally worn out from all the emotional junk and traumatic memories we've walked through this week. I'm weary.

Besides, You, more than anyone, know that walking is a sore subject with me. I looked down at my legs and thought about the number of times in the last thirty years that I'd had to physically relearn to walk—daunting. I'd suffered a broken ankle, torn ligaments in both ankles, and reconstructive surgeries on both ankles. I rotated my ankle and thought about the constant pain I'd suffered both physically and emotionally. The fear of reinjuring a weak joint hovered over me like a black cloud.

Give me a break, God! I had the metal plate removed after my broken ankle less than a year ago. Now You are telling me to walk? What do You mean?

The next morning, on the flight home, I pondered God's instruction to me. I was thrilled to hear His voice again—to know that during our vacation the protective shell around my heart had been shattered. I could now connect with Jim *and* God—but I didn't understand what God was telling me. Was He referring to the physical process of walking, or was He speaking metaphorically, such as to *walk* in a specific direction like ministry, a task, school, or career? Or perhaps He was referring to my spiritual walk, as when Paul directs us to "walk in the spirit and not in the flesh." Or maybe He was referring to my pace—that instead of running through life as I had in the past, He was affirming my desire to slow down and carefully put one foot in front of the other.

God, I'm confused. I prayed. *I want to obey You, but I'm not exactly sure what You mean. Please show me what it means to walk with You.*

THE LONG, SLOW GRIND

"Aren't you finished yet? Why is this taking so long?" I peered over Jim's shoulder as he sat at the lapidary desk, studying the ametrine beneath the bright light.

"The stone is only roughly fashioned," he said.

"Roughly fashioned? I don't understand. It looks like the picture on your pattern," I questioned.

Smiling, Jim removed his head visor loupe and handed it to me.

"Here, take a look at the surface of the stone." He pushed his chair back from the desk and offered me his place. "Look how it reflects light. What does the surface look like to you?" I settled in his chair, positioned the loupe visor and grasped the dop with the ametrine tightly attached to it. Imitating Jim's movements I lifted the stone, held it up to the light, and then moved my head back and forth, closer or further from the stone.

"It sure is hard to get the focal distance just right. You seem to do it so easily." Finally I found the magic spot where everything was in perfect focus. "There, now I can see the surface of a single facet. Wow, it looks like a hardwood floor that hasn't been sanded correctly. It has grooves and tiny divots all over it."

"Honey, that's why it's called *roughly faceted*, because the coarse lap used to create the design leaves a rough, pitted surface on each facet. The edges and meet-points are only crudely defined; it's the best you can do with a coarse lap," Jim said, matter-of-factly.

"Oh, I forgot about the different types of laps."

"I have ten different types of laps. During the grinding phase I use at least three—a coarse one, a medium one, and one that has fine grit. I have to go around the entire cutting sequence for each facet with all three laps."

"All three? Seriously? That's why it takes forever."

"Yes, it's a sloooow process, one that breeds patience."

"Better get crackin' then, buddy." I laughed, as I popped up from his chair and handed him his visor.

Jim unscrewed the center knob and lifted the Frisbee®-looking grinding disc.

"Ewww, what's that milky-looking stuff?" I asked.

"It's the residual grit mixed with water. It's important that none of the coarse grit comes into contact with the stone from this point forward. Before I begin the next round with the next lap, I've got to clean the work area thoroughly to get rid of all residual grit."

I watched for the next ten minutes, as Jim meticulously washed the splash rim and wiped down his entire desk with a wet paper towel and paintbrush.

"Wish my house was dusted and cleaned as well as your workspace." I said jokingly, "Do you hire out?"

As Jim cleaned I flipped through the pages in his notebook of gemstone patterns. "These pages look more like a math book or perhaps a knitting pattern than a gemstone facet design book. How do you know where you are in the pattern? Do you count facets like counting stitches while knitting? I don't see where it identifies when or where to change laps."

"The numbers on the pattern correspond to the dial and a facet on the stone." Jim placed the medium lap into position and turned the knob that secured it in place. He flipped a switch and the lap began to spin. *Grrr… Grrrrr…* He ground one facet then looked at the pattern book and turned the dial to the corresponding number. The stone rotated simultaneously to align the next facet.

"Slowly I'll progress through the entire cutting sequence. This stone has 87 facets; some patterns have 130 facets or more."

"So the more facets, the more brilliant the stone but the more work on your part, right?" I reasoned.

Jim smiled without taking his eyes off the stone. "You got it! Did I mention that this is a slooooow process?" I watched for several more minutes. In that time he'd only completed a few facets.

"This *does* take a long time. I'm going to go work on my oil painting," I said and walked away.

Two hours later the grinding sound stopped. I laid my paintbrush aside and went to Jim's office only to see him washing everything again.

"I thought you were finished?" I said with a hint of disappointment.

"Nope. That's only round two. Now I have to do it all over again with a fine lap. After that I'll repeat the process with a pre-polish lap. Check back with me in a couple of hours."

I rolled my eyes. "I don't think I'd have the patience to be a lapidary. The monotony of doing the same cut over and over would bore me to death. And the rhythmic hum and grind of the machine would put me to sleep."

As Jim wiped down his desk space I asked, "Don't you ever get bored?"

"Nope. Each facet is changed by the touch of the lap. Watching the stone slowly take shape is a thing of beauty." He settled back in his chair and stared intently at the ametrine. I blew him a kiss and went back to painting.

Grrrr… Grrrrrr… Grrrrr…

The sun had set and all was quiet. I went to check on Jim.

"Want to look?" Jim asked, as I entered the room. "Sure!" He placed his visor on my head. I moved my head until I found the "magic spot" in the magnifying glasses. "Ohhh! I can see the

---

Other stones, such as sapphire and topaz, present an additional challenge for the lapidary—the atoms are arranged such that they're softer in one direction than the other. While the softer side makes no difference to the gemstone owner, it creates headaches for the lapidary. During the monotony of shaping and pre-polishing it's easy to forget about the "soft side" and apply the same pressure. Almost instantly you've overcut the facet, and guess what? You have to start over with the sequence.

difference," I squealed. "The surfaces are so smooth—like after a Zamboni® runs across an ice rink. You're done now, right?"

"Yes, with this phase."

"What? This phase?"

"I've only cut about 65% of the stone. I still have to cut the top side and go through the same process with all three laps."

"There are no shortcuts," Jim said firmly. "Every stone most go through the long, slow grind if the brilliance of the light is to be released."

ANATOMY OF A WALK

Slow.

Methodical.

One step at a time.

Over a period of several years, God showed me what He meant when He said, "Walk with me." Certainly He wanted me to slow my pace—to stop running in so many directions so He could free me from my self-fueled adrenaline addiction. He also wanted me to embrace the value of moving forward one slow, incremental step at a time—a type of transformation I'd previously resisted because it seemed tedious. But "walk" referred to something much grander than the mechanics of physically putting one foot in front of the other. "Walk" referred to everything about me in relation to God—what I did, how I thought, how I viewed myself.

"Walk with me" was a call from God to embrace a new lifestyle that required me to trust in Him moment by moment and to live fully in the knowledge that I was His beloved daughter—my true identity. This broad understanding of "walk" meant that, at times, He would also require me to sit in stillness or to stand firm in my convictions.

The walk God called me to would not be easy. It meant facing my past with a present perspective, taking responsibility for my behaviors and trusting His plans for me —even if the plans unfolded in a way that seemed monotonous or boring!

As I studied God's Word, I found amazing similarities between myself and the children of Israel. Like me, God asked them to walk with Him. With Moses as their leader, the Israelites walked away from the bondage of Egypt and into the desert to meet God. The following is a list of five things God seemed to be teaching the children of Israel, and me, as we both learned to walk with Him.

Walk with Me—is to embrace your true identity. For two months the million-or-so Israelites walked...and walked...and walked. Finally they came to Mt. Sinai where God had them sit for two years. In this place He revealed His glory and announced that the children of Israel were His "own special treasure...a kingdom of priests, my holy nation" (Exodus 19:5-6, NLT).

At Mt. Sinai the Israelites were given a new identity. No longer were they called "slave," "rejected," "foreigner." God gave them new names: "free," "beloved," "citizen of God's kingdom."

Likewise, God says to me, a follower of Jesus, "You are a chosen people. You are a kingdom of priests, God's holy nation, his very own possession... ." (1 Peter 2:9, NLT). Sadly, I didn't always embrace the fullness of my noble identity; I was too preoccupied with my self-proclaimed labels: *adrenaline junkie, Jim's wife, mother of two daughters.* Then Jenny died. That rocked my world. Suddenly my identity included *mother of a daughter who died.* I hated this role. I didn't know how to walk in this foreign identity. Some days I'd take a step forward in accepting Jenny's death. The next day I'd fall flat on my face. Other days I'd resort to running sprints away from my painful reality. It's not easy to admit how quickly I'd revert to my drug of choice—adrenaline.

One day we received confirmation that Jim's work would require us to relocate from Alaska to California. God moved us from the land of glaciers to a desert with palm trees. He removed the things and people I'd depended upon, all that was familiar to me.

Grrrr. No one or nowhere to run!

For several years God had me sit. The lack of activity in this desert gave me the space and time to know God more deeply. As I soaked in His presence, God refined my identity. He peeled away my *adrenaline junkie* label and enabled me to accept the label of *mother of a daughter who died*. More importantly, He helped me embrace new names like *daughter of the King* and *beloved*. At age 50 I finally embraced my true identity.

Walk with Me—means letting go. As the Israelites sat at the foot of Mt. Sinai for two years, how did they fill their time? I imagine that for the first few weeks they rested and delighted in their respite from slavery. Then what? Did they sit in their tents "twiddling their thumbs"? What was their purpose? What were they supposed to *do?* God had a plan. He would remove their blemishes and birthmarks through quiet time in His presence and through a transformational walk through the wilderness (Deuteronomy 2:1-3).

But the Israelites struggled to let go of their previous identity. They didn't like their new surroundings. They yearned for the familiarity of Egypt instead of trusting God in the unknown.

When God moved me from Alaska to California, He forced me to walk away from the bondage of an overbooked schedule of work, ministry, service and a constant desire to please others, to an empty schedule of no job, no ministry, no home church, no local friends and a husband who traveled frequently for his work. Initially, I delighted in free time, but after a few weeks I twiddled my thumbs. I felt disconnected and useless. What was my purpose? As I continued to let go of the past I discovered a great truth: God created me as a human *being* not a human *doing.*

Walk with Me—requires a WITH. The importance of this preposition changes everything. We can *walk in, walk out, walk over* or just walk. However, walking *with* someone indicates relationship, an abiding communion. Amos 3:3 (NLT) asks, "Can two people walk together without agreeing on the direction?" The implied answer is *no*. To walk with God means that we agree to walk according to His direction. The Bible assures us that His direction is for our good. Leviticus 26:12 and 13 (NLT) offers these encouraging words:

> I will walk among you; I will be your God, and you will be my people. I, the Lord, am your God, who brought you from the land of Egypt so you would no longer be slaves. I have lifted the yoke of slavery from your neck so you can walk free with your heads held high.

As we walk with Him, He shares His heart, His plans, and even His strength with us. What can be more encouraging to know than this—we do not walk alone!

Walk with Me—requires endurance. God asked the Israelites to walk with Him for forty years. He asks us to walk with Him for a lifetime. Walking can become tiresome; the pace of daily life can exhaust us. But God says that as we look to Him He gives us strength to endure. This was true for the children of Israel; it is true for us as well:

> Though youths grow weary and tired, and vigorous young men stumble badly, yet those who wait for the LORD will gain new strength; They will mount up with wings like eagles, They will run and not get tired, They will walk and not become weary.
>
> (Isaiah 40:30, 31)

Did you notice that the order of the verbs in these verses seems counterintuitive? The natural progression of verbs might be in reverse order: walk, run, and *then* liftoff or soar like an eagle. Pastor Steve Holsinger[5] makes this observation: "The progression is from easiest to hardest...It is easiest to soar and more difficult to walk and not grow weary." Oswald Chambers adds this thought: "There is no thrill for us in walking, yet it is the test for all of our steady and enduring qualities. To 'walk and not faint' is the highest stretch possible as a measure of strength."[6]

This is why we so desperately need God's Spirit. We cannot do life on our own. We need the power of God. His Spirit strengthens us when our human energy wanes. His Spirit enables us to endure, empowers us to go on, and encourages us to not give up. God knows exactly how much we can endure, how much pressure He needs to apply to remove our resistant blemishes. The Apostle Paul endured beatings, imprisonment, shipwrecks, riots, sleepless nights, hunger, and harsh judgments from his critics. He makes this comment about the value of endurance:

> We rejoice in our sufferings, knowing that *suffering produces endurance, and endurance produces character,* and character produces hope, and hope does not put us to shame because God's love has been poured into our hearts through the Holy Spirit who has been given to us.
> (Romans 5:3-5, ESV, emphasis ours)

Walk with Me—is to leave a legacy. As a young girl, I cannot recall any family member modeling what a life of faith and trust in God looks like. Godly role models in my life did not exist. I desire to leave a different legacy than the one I received. After I've been dead for twenty years, I want my children, and my grandchildren, and my great grandchildren to flip through a photo album and say, "That's Nana. She loved Jesus." I want to be remembered as a woman who loved God with all her heart (even when things got tough), who loved and respected her husband (even when it seemed impossible), and who made an effort to be a good mom and grandmother (even when the young'uns didn't understand).

In my late forties I met a woman who was intentional about influencing future generations. Mrs. Howell gave her children and grandchildren a Bible with her handwritten notes and prayers for them, alongside different verses. Her actions inspired me. I purchased a Bible, read it cover to cover, and wrote special notes in the margins for my daughter, Julie. This is a generational keepsake. Long after I'm gone, my words, and God's Word, will continue to challenge Julie, and her children, and her children's children to walk with God.

What about you? Is God challenging you to stop listening to the world's lies and embrace your true identity as a child of the King? Is He asking you to let go of your past so you can embrace your future? Is He asking you to stop running ahead, or lagging behind, and simply walk *with* Him? Is there a situation you need to endure so that He can shape your character? Does He want you to be intentional about the legacy you leave?

God wants us to walk, just walk with Him. Walk with Him on smooth, sandy beaches. Walk with Him up steep mountains. Walk with Him through dark valleys.

Put one foot in front of the other; take the next step—steps that are sometimes difficult. But always remain confident because we can trust the One with whom we walk.

My prayer for you, dear friend, is that you will not get discouraged or grow weary. Walk with God, slow and steady. Listen for His still, quiet voice that lovingly says, **"Walk with Me."**

2 GEMS

PRAYER:

Abba Father, my desire is to walk with You. Please give me the willingness to walk at Your pace and the ability to let go of my adrenaline-fueled lifestyle. Help me to depend upon Your Spirit to provide my daily endurance. Let me walk in knowledge that Your pace and path are perfect. Let my daily walk with You be a beautiful reflection for generations to come.

God can change me through a process—one step at a time.

In the daily grind:

- Pray for endurance, steadfastness and peace.
- Walk in the Light. (John 12:35)
- Walk by faith. (2 Corinthians 5:7)
- Let go of the things that weigh you down.
- Walk with God, at His pace and according to His direction.

CHAPTER

The Scream of Surrender

"JENNY, WANT TO go for a hike?"

"Sure, Dad," my seventeen-year-old chirped. "Let me grab some shoes."

Really?! Her cheerful acceptance both thrilled and stunned me.

It had been two years since our last hike together. When Jenny was young, hiking had been our "daddy/daughter" time. Together we'd explored the Alaska Chugach Mountains, which offered breathtaking views of jagged, snow-packed peaks lapped by an icy ocean. But when Jenny entered high school, swimming, softball, and other activities took priority. An emotional wedge crept between us. Strange new girlfriends and boys became her focus—friends sporting tattoos, body piercings, and discourteous manners alien to our family.

She'd begun to defy house rules. She lived on the outer boundaries of grace and often tested the borders, which created tension between her and her sister Julie, and between Jana and me.

Her rebellion initially surfaced in small ways—forbidden flips on the family trampoline, unapproved visits to a friend's house, and curfew violations. I dismissed her behavior, thinking *she's just a spirited kid being a kid.* Jana viewed her actions as alarming precursors of disobedience...and Jana was right.

153

Now, at 17, "hand-to-hand combat" best described our daily interactions. In recent months she'd snuck out of the house, attended wild parties, and experimented with drugs. Darkness brooded over her.

A chasm spanned between us that barred communication and shut down parental respect. She trampled our precious relationship with frequent lies and dishonor. I missed her carefree laugh and her simple trust and obedience.

I missed my little girl.

I ached for the days when we'd romp the mountain slopes together. Today she'd agreed to share time with me. A thought entered my mind—hers too, I believe. *Let's do this! We may never get another chance.* And indeed, it proved to be our last hike.

The first leg of the hike required a trek through spruce and alder woodlands—difficult to traverse, humid, and bug-infested. Because of the 80-degree heat that July day, we donned short pants and T-shirts, a decision that later proved unwise. The heat brought out the bugs.

"I miss Rudy," Jenny said as she swatted at a mosquito. "It's sad to be here without him."

"I miss him too, Sweetie." We lamented the absence of our golden retriever who was now too arthritic to join us. Agreement between us felt good, even on something as small as this. With each step my heart grew cautiously optimistic toward a restoration of our battered and scarred relationship.

Dense, waist-high ferns released clouds of spores that dusted our clothes rusty-red, leaving a bitter, acrid taste in our mouths. Mossy, rotten logs and other fallen timber slowed our progress. This leg of the trip was no fun, but we pressed up the steep slope and on to timberline where the humid, buggy woodlands would give way to cool, refreshing winds that swept the treeless, arctic ridge lines.

"Dad! A moose!" Jenny yelled.

A large bull stood his ground in a clearing about 100 yards up the slope. Jenny hated moose—she'd been chased several times before. *No way to outpace him if he charges us in this thick brush.* Jenny wanted to turn back, but I yearned to press on and enjoy these precious moments together.

"He won't bother us if we keep our distance," I reassured her... and myself. She clutched my arm as we detoured cross-slope. Swarms of horseflies and deerflies pestered the animal in the suffocating undergrowth. Cautiously, we passed safely around the majestic antlered bull.

After two hours we finally approached timberline. The hillside steepened to a 45-degree slope. The vegetation thinned. Drenched with sweat, we stopped every 100 feet of elevation change to catch our breath. No breeze stirred the silent forest. I led the way; Jenny followed close behind. She had removed her T-shirt and wore only her sports top.

Miss Buff, I thought, as she grinned and gave me a Rambo flex.

One last rest stop and we're out of these buggy woods.

We paused a moment—a final rest stop at the woodland's edge before our welcomed escape into the open terrain. We could sense the cool, fresh breeze filtering into the underbrush.

Suddenly, time became mysteriously distorted. Our actions seemed in slow motion. I experienced two bizarre sensations simultaneously—the incessant humming of horseflies against the hush of the forest and a powerful blistering pain in my right ankle and heel that left me woozy. I struggled to comprehend the mystery. In seemingly slow time-lapse I turned around to see Jenny swatting the horseflies in long, slow strokes.

Why so many?

I looked down. Five hornets pumped searing venom into my ankle, stinging it simultaneously. My right foot stood on top of their nest. A fiery cloud of angry hornets enshrouded us.

Should I stand still… or move my foot and release more of the devils from their nest? Brain won't function… thoughts blurred… Each second crawled by. We both seemed unable to move—frozen in a stunned stupor.

The only interruption to the dreadful buzzing was the fiery *pop!* from each hornet as it flew into and stung exposed flesh. I stood up-slope, on top of the nest. Jenny, five feet behind me and lower on the slope, stood with her face and chest immersed in the fog of hornets. I watched her flinch repeatedly as they popped her bare skin.

And then a horrible sight. Jenny slowly lowered her arms and became rigid as she succumbed to the endless swarm of insects and their maddeningly painful stings.

"Daddy! Help me!" she whimpered in a quaking voice.

Her cry jarred me into action.

Instinctively, I lunged and knocked her backwards, and we rolled thirty yards down the steep, brushy slope. We clambered to our feet and ran another 75 yards downhill through the brush. Our retreat confused and lost the last of the hornets.

We stopped in a small clearing.

"I… hurt… all over, I hurt." Jenny's shoulders shook with sobs. We both trembled from pain, fear, and adrenalin. I held her in my arms and felt her breaths come as short, raspy gasps. Another terror struck.

Jana is allergic to bee stings. Had Jenny ever been stung? Certainly not to this extent. Oh God, if she's allergic to stings, this will kill her!

Because of her self-harming choices, Jana and I wondered if Jenny would survive her high school years. *Lord, is this how You plan to end her life? Please protect her!*

I set us both down on a fallen, mossy log to calm her. Scenes from the movie *My Girl* flashed through my mind. *A young blonde-haired boy swatting hornets dies as he succumbs to their fatal stings. Would that be Jenny's fate?* She'd received over thirty-five stings; I had at least twenty. We couldn't call for help—we were out of emergency cell phone range. Besides, a rescue flight could never reach us on this slope. Could I carry her out of these woods?

I embraced her welt-covered shoulders with my left arm and used my right hand to pick twigs and spruce needles from her long blonde hair. She shivered.

"We'll be fine once we get off this mountain," I assured her. I studied her face, her stings, looking for signs of an allergic reaction. *Thank you, God, she's going to be okay.*

"What about the moose?" she asked in a trembling voice. *Oh, the stupid moose—how trivial that seems after being stung half to death.*

"He'll be long gone by now," I answered. She remained nestled in my arms for a few precious minutes. Jenny's cry for help and her surrender to my embrace melted the years of distance between us. It's what I'd longed for...this moment. I smiled into her eyes. I was her daddy. She was my little girl. *God, let this moment live forever.*

PRESSURE THAT PERFECTS
Skreeeeech!

The scream from our ametrine is piercing, eerie—almost human. This is the scream of surrender as the final facet, the top table facet of the ametrine, yields to the pressure of polishing. Polishing is both a difficult and exhilarating step of gemstone crafting because it transforms each facet into a mirrored surface—a window to display the brilliance and color of the stone. The other steps are preparatory; the polish unveils the beauty of the gem. Polishing requires intense pressure—up to several hundred pounds per square inch. And with the crushing pressure comes amazing transformation.

As a lapidary, I must know the individual qualities of each stone I polish; different stones require different methods. Sapphire and amethyst require different polishing techniques, polishing compounds, and pressure. Sometimes I even modify techniques between two of the same type of garnets. Polishing is a mysterious and variable process—it's driven by the uniqueness of each stone and the skilled eye of the lapidary. Some lapidaries are satisfied with the first flash of light and leave the minor blemishes behind. Others, like me, prefer a perfectly polished surface. To see the residual blemishes is another challenge.

Viewing the defects on an almost-polished facet is an art unto itself. A glance at the reflecting surface under strong magnification is blinding. The tricky part is rotating the surface slightly, just off the plane of reflected light. It's a tiny angle of adjustment. The flash "blinks off," leaving a dark surface, but it's still near enough to the reflection angle to expose tiny defects and scratches. It takes me

---

The technical explanation for how a metal lap, polishing compound, and great pressure create a mirror-like polish remains a mystery. Several complex theories exist. Regardless, as these three entities converge on a facet, the surface undergoes a beautiful transformation.

Gemstone polishing is more art than science. Various stone types (quartz, sapphire, and garnet) respond differently to the pressure of polishing. Some stones polish easily; some are difficult. Different lap materials (steel, zinc, ceramic) perform better with different stones. Polishing compounds usually include finely ground diamond or sapphire with face powder consistency. Each lapidary has his own techniques, style, and equipment preferences. The common variable is incredible pressure.

three to four cycles of polishing and examination to remove the last blemish from a facet. *Sometimes the final trace of a stubborn blemish requires the greatest pressure.*

Finally, the facet is completed—a flawless, mirrored surface. No more pressure is required. *You can't polish a polish.* A strange relief floods over me; it's a peculiar satisfaction, a beautiful increment of completed work.

Polishing removes the hazy finish on a stone's facets and releases its true brilliance. *Likewise, the blemishes of sinful self in our lives are polished away by God, the Master Lapidary, so that we can reflect His light.*

Polishing begins as the lapidary presses a pre-polished facet against the spinning lap. Only slight pressure (2-3 pounds per square <u>inch</u>, or "psi") is necessary. Although seemingly insignificant, such force applied to a tiny square facet (2 mm by 2 mm—a miniscule fraction of a square inch) equates to about 350 to 500 psi! No wonder transformation occurs.

Finally, a linear blemish often emerges out of nowhere. Some speculate that this blemish is caused by internal damage to the crystal structure by a coarse grain of grit during the grind or pre-polish. Regardless, the pits must be removed through one or more cycles of polishing.

REMOVING THE BLEMISH OF SELF

Consider the similarities between the process I follow as a human lapidary and how God, the Master Lapidary, works in our lives to make us more like Christ:

- Both the Master Lapidary and the human lapidary use different polishing techniques, depending on the nature of the gem.
- The polishing process follows a consistent sequence of steps.
- We each respond differently to the pressure of polishing.
- Like the stone on the lap, we scream as the Lapidary applies intense pressure to remove our final blemishes.

As living stones, we scream because polishing hurts...badly! Fiery polishing drives us to the border of an unknown territory—a new and frightening place of unfamiliar circumstances and emotions—a land called "Self-Surrender." God yearns to hear our scream, not because of some perverse pleasure in watching us suffer, but because the scream signals that we're finally ready to look to the Almighty for help. "Self" has failed and we've reached our endpoint, "the end of our rope." We genuinely seek a Higher Authority who will accept our burdens...One to trust instead of self.

But it doesn't come easy.

Polishing is often camouflaged within crises that either strike us personally or that afflict our family, friends, and other loved ones. Even though God has a clear plan about how He will use these situations to remove our blemishes of self, we don't always understand what is happening or *why* it's happening.

Jana and I experienced tremendous emotional conflict as we individually dealt with Jenny's rebellion in our own way. We couldn't seem to get on the same page. And we didn't understand why God would allow such a thing in the life of those who love and serve Him.

THE SCREAM OF SURRENDER

Confounding thoughts flooded our minds. *We raised Jenny well. I (Jana) was a stay-at-home mom. I (Jim) taught her Bible stories and baptized her. What happened to the old proverb, "Train up a child in the way he should go (Proverbs 22:6)"?... We did it right; how could she rebel?*

Others have pondered similar mysteries. Let's look at a verse that offers some insight about how to face situations which, on the surface, make no sense:

> Beloved, *do not be surprised* at the fiery ordeal among you...as though some strange thing were happening to you.
>
> (1 Peter 4:12, emphasis ours)

Interesting.

According to Scripture we should not be surprised when fiery trials cross our path. Instead, Scripture implies that trials should be expected; these trials serve a purpose that's defined in the remainder of the passage:

> Beloved, do not be surprised at the fiery ordeal among you, which comes upon you *for your testing*, as though some strange thing were happening to you; but to the degree that *you share the sufferings of Christ*, keep on rejoicing, so...you may rejoice with exultation.
>
> (1 Peter 4:12, 13, emphasis ours)

Therein lays the key. The "fiery ordeal" and the "strange thing" are not random, chaotic events, or punishment by an angry God. Rather, they're permitted by God for two beneficial purposes:

- To test us
- To enable us to share in the sufferings of Christ

These two truths comprise a hallowed cleft of reason and hope while the rest of our world crumbles away. They reveal a Divine purpose at work in our life that offers encouragement and deserves further scrutiny. In this chapter we'll look at the benefits of testing; in the next two chapters we'll explore the benefits of sharing in Christ's sufferings. As we sift these sacred truths of polishing, prayerfully ask God to reveal the purpose behind your personal ordeal.

THE BENEFITS OF TESTING

Proverbs 17:3 says, "The refining pot is for silver and the furnace for gold, but the Lord tests hearts." You ponder: *Why would God test me? He already knows everything about me, right?* Yes. But the test is not for God's benefit; the test comes so we can learn something about ourselves.

Scripture makes it clear that no one escapes tests. Even Jesus experienced testing. The Pharisees challenged His claim as the Divine Son with frequent cunning traps (Matthew 16:1; 9:13; John 8:6). Jesus' response to each test revealed His grace, wisdom, and authority—in other words, His true nature as God Incarnate.

How can testing benefit us? Let us suggest three ways: First, testing reveals my true nature; second, testing draws me to God; third, testing produces godly character. Let's examine each of these more closely within the context of Scripture.

TESTING REVEALS MY TRUE NATURE.

Two men once endured an identical, horribly painful test at exactly the same time and yet completed it with entirely opposite results. Intrigued?

Two thieves were crucified alongside Jesus, one on his right, another on his left. Initially both thieves joined the chief priests and scribes in "casting...insult at Him."[1] But one thief's true nature emerged during the torment of suffering. The horrific pain of the nails in his wrists and feet drove him to the brink of unconsciousness.

His breath came in shortened gasps, and he knew that death was only a few hours away. The terrible deeds of his life flashed through his mind, and a grim reality set in: He was wicked and destined for hell. In that helpless condition, the thief confronted his own sin and acknowledged his guilt with a full change of heart.

And then an amazing thing—he rebuked the other thief for insulting Christ. "Do you not even fear God... we indeed are suffering justly, for *we are receiving what we deserve* for our deeds; but *this man has done nothing wrong*"[2] (emphasis ours).

The thief struggled to turn toward the center cross and begged the Lord, "Jesus, remember me when You come in Your kingdom!"

Jesus replied, "Truly I say to you, today you shall be with Me in Paradise."[3]

Suffering exposed two thieves' hearts. One cried out in surrender and passed the test. Scripture provides no record that the other thief ever acknowledged his own sinful nature.

Suffering polishes away deception so we can view ourselves, and Christ, more clearly.

TESTING DRAWS ME CLOSER TO GOD.

Jairus desperately searched for Jesus in hopes that the Great Rabbi would come and heal his dying daughter. *Where is He? Will there be enough time to save her?* His despair intensified with each dusty step: *Will I see my daughter alive again?* Finally, he spotted a crowd—and Jesus. "Jairus... fell at His feet and implored Him earnestly... please come and lay Your hands on her, so that she will get well."[4]

Jesus, and the crowd, departed with Jairus. *So many people... so slow.*

Suddenly a woman who sought healing from internal bleeding touched Jesus. While Jesus tended to the woman someone delivered the dreaded news to Jairus, "Your daughter has died; why trouble the Teacher anymore?"[5]

Cruel words spoken to a bleeding heart.

Why God!? *You chose to stop and heal the woman; now it's too late for my daughter.*

Jesus replied with calming words to the aching father: "Do not be afraid any longer, only believe."[6]

Jesus went to Jairus' home where He performed an even greater miracle than healing sickness—He raised Jairus' daughter from the dead.[7]

Can you imagine the emotions Jarius experienced towards Jesus in that moment? Can you picture the unfathomable gratitude, the reverential awe that he felt towards the One who restored warmth to his daughter's cold flesh? Can you envision the intimate love that filled his heart as he considered the One who answered his desperate cry for help?

I can only dream and fleetingly imagine the first two of these emotions, but I've experienced the third. I've never felt closer to Jesus than the five days following Jenny's death. I could feel His hands support me, His breath sustain me, His mysterious peace comfort and carry me through the darkest hours of my life. It was a level of intimacy I've since craved yet fear to relive. Indeed, testing forges an intimacy with Jesus in a way that only the crushed in spirit can comprehend.

TESTING PRODUCES GODLY CHARACTER.

Paul suffered greatly in the Lord's service. Five times he received thirty-nine lashes. Three times he was beaten with rods. Three times he was shipwrecked. He was stoned, imprisoned, and shackled. He suffered emotionally from threats of death and from slander by those in the very churches he founded. How did he benefit from his tests? He writes:

> I have learned to be content in whatever circumstances I am. I know how to get along with humble means, and I also know how to live in prosperity; in any and every circumstance I have learned the secret of being filled and going hungry, both of having abundance and suffering need.
> (Philippians 4:11, 12)

Paul learned contentment through his ordeals. Scripture speaks of other character traits that come through testing: endurance (James 1:2, 3), humility (Deuteronomy 8:16), and purity (Psalms 26:2). How badly do we yearn for these virtues?

I have a precious friend who exhibits mighty faith. When my faith wanes, his faith strengthens me. Witty, kind, and extremely intelligent, he lives alone in a small apartment—deaf and legally blind. He walks a two-mile route to and from work, even on the icy roads during January's cold, dark days. He trusts God for protection from traffic mishaps, foul play, and the moose encounters. His cheery outlook and tenacious perseverance humble me—such faith and godly character only blossom through the rigor of severe testing.

Testing reveals our true nature. It draws us to Jesus, and it changes our character, as it polishes away self and allows us to reflect the light of God. Certainly, the pressure of polishing *is* hard. But can you begin to understand His purpose?

God has not abandoned you, nor is He carelessly testing your "grit" to watch you snap. He is not punishing you. The Master Lapidary *must* lovingly press each of us onto the spinning lap—His love demands it. Just as my restoration occurred with Jenny during those precious few minutes after our hornet stings, testing bridges the gap between us and God. When we turn to our Father and cry out, "Daddy, help me," He gathers us in His arms. The pain diminishes as we surrender to the comfort of His loving embrace.

COMFORT WHEN TESTED

As a living stone, you may never comprehend the blemish that God is painfully polishing away. You may never understand His timing or His methods. The pressure may seem crushingly unbearable.

But did you know that He equips us to bear the pain of polishing?

"How" you may ask, "when the pain hurts so badly?"

The answers are tucked away in the Word, penned by two apostles who were very familiar with the fiery tests of polishing—Paul and Peter. In Romans 5:2, Paul had just affirmed that he "exults in hope of the glory of God." The Greek word for "exult" means to joyfully boast, rejoice, glorify. His next statement is deep:

> And not only this, but we also *exult in our tribulations*, knowing that tribulation brings about perseverance; and perseverance, proven character; and proven character, hope; and hope does not disappoint, because the love of God has been poured out within our hearts through the Holy Spirit who was given to us.
>
> (Romans 5:3-5, emphasis ours)

Have you spent much time "exulting" in your tribulations?

We hadn't. By the time Paul wrote this letter to the Romans he had been rejected, beaten, shipwrecked, and stoned.

Was Paul delusional? Was his description of "joyful boasting"[8] honestly sincere? What happened to Paul?

Notice that Paul's "exultation" *began* with tribulations, but it *concluded* with a stable, non-disappointing hope, "*because the love of God has been poured out within our hearts...*"[9] (emphasis ours).

Cleary, Paul's heart had been changed. God's love had replaced Paul's anger, hopelessness, and doubts. How? The process is described here:

After you have *suffered* for a *little while*, the God of all grace, who called you to His eternal glory in Christ, *will* Himself perfect, confirm, strengthen *and* establish you.
(1 Peter 5:10, emphasis ours)

Do you see it? After we have "suffered for a little while" we *will be changed*. There are no "ifs, ands, or buts" or any other qualifiers in His promise. We *will* be changed after we have suffered for a little while. And it's a change that greatly impacts our character for good.

Notice that Peter did *not* say our *circumstances* will change—many times they do, but not always—rather, the *heart* will change. God Himself will change us and bring perfection, which includes joy instead of anger; and confirmation, which includes confidence and hope instead of hopelessness. You get the idea. God's love will be "poured out into our hearts" just as it was with Paul.

THE CRY GOD YEARNS TO HEAR

How do we release the splendor of God that echoes in heaven and reverberates throughout the earth? *It begins with the cry for help from a heart surrendered to Him.*

Emotions of all colors wash over me as I reflect on my mountain hike with Jenny and her plea, "Daddy, help me." Her cry of surrender bridged the relational chasm between us. Her plea forged unity. It triggered my immediate response to rescue and comfort her.

Glory thunders from a feeble cry in the land called Self Surrender. In this, God is greatly glorified.

What about you? Have you surrendered to God? Have you cried out to Him for help? Your prayers, your pondering, your pleas—even the time spent reading this book—testify that you recognize the flaws and limitations of "self."

God's heart rejoices when you cry out in surrender. Your scream sends Him into action. You are His unique, precious stone, and He's crazy about you!

Of this you can be certain: God works through your tests and your surrender to transform you into Christ's image. His pure light beams forth—light that reveals His glory and illuminates, even to the ends of the earth.

2 GEMS

PRAYER:

Lord, I've tried to live life in my own strength. It hasn't worked. In this moment I surrender everything to You—my heart, my mind, my fiercely stubborn will. I surrender my hopes and dreams. I release my expectations and my need for control. I withhold nothing...I abandon myself completely to You. In all things, dear Lord, not my will...but Yours.

Absolute surrender brings glory to God.

- The lapidary delights in the scream of a stone being polished because it means the stone has nearly reached perfection. Similarly God delights in the scream of a "living stone" who surrenders completely to Him because it means that His work is being accomplished.

- Sometimes we are tested. Testing draws us closer to God, develops Christlike character in our lives, and reveals our true nature.

- God wants us to exult in our trials because He uses them to "polish" and perfect us.

CHAPTER

Absolute Surrender

THIS CHAPTER MAY not be for you.

If, for example, you've never screamed accusations at God during a prolonged crisis, then skip this chapter.

If you've never uttered from a pit of darkness, "God, if You really are good and You love me, why don't You end this misery?" then move ahead.

If you've never clung with bleeding fingernails to the sovereignty of God—the belief that He is the Divine Ruler of the Universe whose plans and actions towards you are perfect and good—and felt your confidence in Him slip away, then advance to Chapter Ten.

But keep reading if you've ever screamed, "God, I'm scared spitless of You and I struggle to trust You as a Father anymore!" Press on if incessant trials have provoked such deep anger that you demand a face-to-face showdown with the Creator Himself to explain His actions. And keep reading if, at times, God's justice seems laughable—the wicked continue to flourish while others, like you who serve Him faithfully, are pounded into dust.

It seems to us that certain individuals and families are singled out by God and destined to suffer loss upon loss, crisis upon crisis, and blow upon blow. Sure, a few trials are preventable, and those who stumble have learned and grown through those experiences. They've fully surrendered in every way they know how and yet they can't escape this haunting reality—the trials just keep coming...and coming...and coming.

Many who experience such seemingly "never-ending" trauma eventually reach a breaking point. Confused, crushed, and worn out, doubts about God's character begin to surface and swirl in their once-confident faith. *How could a "good God" who designed the universe, who could stop this chaos with a single word, just sit there and do nothing?* Prayer was once something to bank on, but now even it seems futile. *Why should I pray? What can I pray? My prayers have no effect—does God even listen to me?*

Please understand this: We are *not* speaking here about people who give up, curse God, and leave their faith. Rather, we are talking about devoted Christians who are broken, crushed, and deeply wounded, and they simply cannot conceive of a reason why their Father continues to allow such pain.

This may describe you—angry at God by His seeming indifference to your suffering, doubtful of His very nature, and pondering if He really even cares.

If so, this chapter *is* for you.

Dear friend, we know it may be hard to believe that even when your world is collapsing God's sovereignty remains firmly anchored. Though your life feels out of control, He is firmly in control. His love for you stands rock solid. And there *is* a reason behind your suffering. He did *not* make a mistake, nor has He abandoned you, even though every strand in your being screams otherwise.

I understand.

I know how it feels to be slammed over and over to the point that you just don't care—and you honestly question if God cares either. The time was about two years before Jenny died and everything in my life was in shambles.

MY BREAKING POINT

It was 9 a.m. in Anchorage on a chilly spring morning. I (Jim) sat alone in my toasty car in the parking lot at my workplace. Even though a glorious flood of spring sunbeams heated the car's interior, I shivered with dread and anger at the traumas that tormented us and the task that lay ahead.

Our marriage was fractured. Jana and I had become strongly polarized over how to discipline our drug-abusing daughter. Now the two of us locked horns on most any Jenny-related topic, and each conversation seemed to end with a chilly, stressful silence. We were still licking our wounds from a month earlier when we'd enforced tough love with Jenny to help her change her ways. Instead of submitting to our household boundaries, she'd moved out—and it broke our hearts.

Our finances burdened us like a lead weight. Jana had been laid off from her job, and we were still playing catch-up from a backlog of debt accrued during my job loss a few years prior.

Work was extremely stressful. My current job required that I make decisions without the appropriate training while lacking sufficient staff to execute the projects. My job stressed me; Jana's lack of a job stressed her; an onslaught of medical bills stressed us both.

And then again, there was Jenny. We were in our fourth year of battles with a teenager who had blossomed into a physical beauty adorned by full-blown rebellion. Our latest gasoline credit card statement showed over $1,000 in unauthorized charges in one month. The company told us that we must either pay the balance or press charges against the thief. We heartily agreed to press charges since Jenny emphatically swore she had nothing to do with the purchases.

Then the phone call earlier this morning. The credit card company explained that cameras at the gas station had captured video of a young woman with long blonde hair making gas purchases for other people in exchange for payments in cash. We knew from their descriptions that it was Jenny—she had found another way to support herself and her drug habit.

And now I faced the task of pressing charges against my own unstable and floundering daughter. What should I do? We really couldn't afford to pay the charges, but if I didn't pay them she could be sent to prison. In her current state she could never survive a hostile prison environment. In my mind, sending her to prison equated to her death sentence.

I sat in the car for over twenty minutes screaming at God.

"You've gone too far! Why are you picking on us? Leave us alone!" I pounded the steering wheel with my fist. "Why would you ask me to kill my own child?"

And then, God's quiet voice spoke to me ever so softly, ***"I asked the same of Abraham. Do you really trust Me? Release her to Me."***

This was the climax of four years of misery—a pinnacle moment heralded by my fearful shivering in a warm, cozy car over my grave concern for Jenny. It was an iconic, cataclysmic contrast rooted in the very character of God. I had come face to face with the gracious "loving" Father, but I stood spiritually terrified by His "sovereignty" that would stop at nothing to force me to release Jenny into His hands.

We'd labored all our married lives to follow and obey God. And this was His response—relentless pounding with situations we could no longer bear? I felt like a small sailboat on a dark, raging sea, randomly blown about by terrifying winds; helpless, with no direction, waiting for the next crashing wave to utterly destroy us.

It was the straw that broke the camel's back. My confidence in God's character had been shattered.

Yet even during these dark moments, the distant tones of Scripture formed a perplexing harmony in the black cavern of hopelessness that filled my soul: "For I know the plans I have for you...plans for welfare and not calamity, to give you a future and a hope"[1]..."My ways are higher than your ways and My thoughts than your thoughts."[2]

Those faint, confounding tones formed a tiny strand of hope that threaded its way through the putrid muck which defined my world. A thread of mysterious inner strength bolstered my fainting soul. The tiny strand of strength certainly didn't come from my inner being. I had nothing. I was utterly spent.

Instead, it was a subtle reminder that, even though it felt as if God had abandoned me, He was still there. And despite my confusion and frustration that He would allow such pain and force such gut-wrenching demands, if God really was there, then a glimmer of hope still existed.

ISOLATED BUT NOT ALONE

I stand at my lapidary table keenly aware of the decision before me.

It's time. I must let go.

For a short duration I must separate myself from this ametrine I have so painstakingly fashioned. Separation is not an option—it's the only way to release the full brilliance of this particular stone.

Here's the problem: A layer of wax is smeared over the facets, so thick that it cannot simply be wiped away with a soft towel. This wax initially served a purpose—it secured the ametrine to the dop so I could shape the stone. But now that the stone is perfectly formed and polished, and I've removed it from the dop, the wax is no longer needed. It must be stripped away.

I pour methanol into a small clear jar. Sickly sweet fumes engulf my tabletop workspace and permeate the room. I set the jar on the lapidary table, slowly lower the gem into the liquid, and then release it.

The solvent quickly performs its aggressive task. The clear liquid turns dirty brown as, layer by layer, the methanol strips away the reddish, waxy residue.

For a moment, let's imagine that our ametrine is alive—that it can think, feel, and speak. How would it respond to being dropped in the solvent?

Surely it would scream, "Why have you abandoned me?" Such a response would be understandable. For the first time this stone is in foreign surroundings, isolated from me and all the stabilizing influences it has ever known. No longer is it safely secured to the dop. No longer is it guided by my firm and reassuring hand. No longer does it sense progression, purpose, and the hope of transformation. Instead, it's confused. Alone. Helplessly trapped within a small jar and surrounded by a heavy fog of hostile solvent where it is relentlessly attacked and stripped. Nothing makes sense…darkness closes in…despair descends as the relentless solvent churns away.

The gem sits in this state of hopelessness; it has no idea that honor and brilliance wait just outside the jar's thin glass walls. It will emerge from the liquid purified, radiant, and ready to receive the grand mounting I have selected to show off its brilliance.

If this were indeed a "living stone" that could think and feel, I would speak these words of comfort: "Don't fret, little gem. This brief trial is preparing for you a future glory that will make your suffering worthwhile. Though you cannot understand my actions, trust that they are necessary. Though you cannot see me, believe that I am here…watching…waiting…anticipating the radiance that will be yours."

THE PINNACLE OF ALL SURRENDERS

Surrender.

We've talked about the need to surrender to God throughout this book, and we've wandered over the stony foothills of surrender, but a mountain lies ahead. Have you ever considered that different levels of surrender might exist?

Think about one of your early trials. You trusted God. You knew that He was present with His hand underneath to catch you if you fell. And He faithfully delivered you.

Then came another level of surrender. You faithfully trusted God through a particularly painful trial. Perhaps things ended differently than you'd hoped, but you survived, right?

But what happened when you were forced to wallow in black, putrid mire over and over and over again? What if we're so battered by wave after wave of crises that we have no strength to even grasp at God's hand? Isn't that an entirely different level of surrender?

And what if He withdraws His hand altogether? We would gladly surrender—but to Whom, and for what? *Is it possible to surrender even further to One who has, according to all the evidence you perceive, abandoned you?*

Dear friend, this is the deepest level of surrender, the equivalent of being placed in the solvent where everything you know as safe and true is stripped from you...where even God Himself seemingly turns His back and walks away.

Authors of diverse theological backgrounds have recognized and labeled this deeper level of surrender. Consider these themes:

- Unconditional surrender (Charles Spurgeon, 1876)[3]
- Surrender of "secret attachments" (Thomas Merton, 1961)[4]
- Absolute surrender (Andrew Murray, 1981)[5]
- Radical dependence (George Barna, 2011)[6]

Each author notes an initial surrender, which includes the "giving up of sins" (Merton), or the initial recognition of the "end of self" (Murray); however, all four authors focus on a second level of surrender that Barna describes as "complete brokenness...a radical dependence upon God."

These authors also note that God *leads us* toward this unconditional surrender. Murray states, "God accomplishes your surrender," but he later clarifies that He does so "through our surrender," or our willingness to let Him work within us. Merton speaks of God's removal of our secret attachments—our imperfections of which we are blind—by His hands, "working...in the night of aridity and suffering," while working through our willingness. Despite God's efforts, *Barna concludes from his national surveys that less than 4 percent of U.S. "born again Christians" fully surrender and experience radical dependence upon God.*

Really? Only 4 percent? That's stunning, and one must ask, "Why?"

Could "self" really be so resilient? It naturally leads us to ponder that if so few *willingly* surrender, then does God attempt to force us by "bludgeoning us to death" with trial after trial until the 4 percent finally scream, "Enough! I give up!"? In that case, did the other 96 percent successfully resist God's efforts?

Or perhaps there's something different going on. Perhaps these 4 percent were not singled out for "bludgeoning" but for honor. Perhaps there's a higher plan at work in which God qualifies them through suffering to fulfill a special purpose in His Kingdom and a sacred place close to His heart. *Perhaps this was God's plan all along, that these select few experience God's character on a deeper level and dwell with Him in such intimate relationship that it equips them for a greater service than ever imaginable.*

Let's explore these possibilities in the life of a blameless man whom God allowed to be crushed to powder.

JOB: CRUSHED BEYOND RECOGNITION

What follows is the story of Job, as written in Scripture, with a bit of my own interpretation and imagination tossed in. I'll share the story and then draw some principles that will help us form a new perspective of suffering at its deepest level.

The account begins with "life as usual" for Job. However, Job is completely unaware that he's the object of a spirited dialogue in heaven. It begins with God bragging about Job to Satan.

"Have you considered My servant Job?" the Lord said to Satan, For there is no one like him on the earth, a *blameless and upright* man, fearing God and turning away from evil"[7] (emphasis ours).

"*Of course* Job is blameless," Satan immediately shot back, "because You made a hedge about him, a protective wall by the work of Your hands. You blessed the work of his hands. But if You touch all that he has he will surely curse You to Your face"[8] (emphasis ours).

So it began: a challenge established—a test in the heavenlies between God and Satan—a contest played out in the life of a helpless human man on earth.

Why? Why did God agree to such a test?

Satan's challenge was an opportunity for God to silence the devil's boasting while simultaneously affirming to all angelic realms watching the drama unfold, and to future mankind, that He alone is the Sovereign Ruler of the Universe. It was also a chance for God to reveal Himself to Job and to refine Job's character to yet another level of righteousness.

God gave Satan permission to test Job, and He allowed Satan to establish the winning criterion for the test: "He will surely curse You to Your face." In other words, "If he curses You, I win; if not, You win." But before Satan went to work destroying Job, God made a stipulation:

"Behold, all that he has is in your power, only do not put forth your hand on him"[9] (emphasis ours).

ROUND 1: SATAN STRIPS JOB OF HIS POSSESSIONS AND FAMILY.

Satan went to work destroying Job. He robbed him of his livelihood (his job). He dispersed his possessions and killed his family (all of his sons and daughters—except his wife).[10] Job's shock and grief must have mounted unimaginably as messengers arrived hourly, each with horrifying news: "Your sons and daughters are all dead." "Your livestock has been stolen; nothing is left." "The people who worked for you have all been killed."

What was happening? This could be no mere coincidence.

Job's reaction?

Shock. Agony. Grief.

A perplexing storm of gut-wrenching emotions swirled through the deepest recesses of Job's soul. He sensed the strange calmness of spiritual presence on one hand and a vast canyon of black desolation on the other. His life's resources, gone. His servants and friends who supported him and managed his possessions, wiped away. But these losses were nothing compared to the death of his children—not just one son or one daughter, but all *ten* children born of his seed were lost in a single day!

In the midst of incredible grief Job fell down, worshipped God, and made an astounding statement that set the bar of faith high—even on heaven's doorstep itself—for all generations to come: "The Lord gave and the Lord has taken away. Blessed be the name of the Lord."[11]

The enormity of that statement thundered through the hallways of heaven and deafened Satan's ears. An immediate roar of angelic praise battered him even further as it became clear that God had won the contest. Through all his suffering, Job did not sin nor did he blame God.[12]

Satan lost…he swore…he fumed…and yet, undeterred, he planned another test for Job.

ROUND 2: SATAN STRIPS JOB OF HIS HEALTH.
Once again, a heavenly scene. Satan approached God.

"Skin for skin!…all that a man has he will give for his life. However, put forth Your hand now, and touch his bone and his flesh; he will curse You to Your face."[13]

In effect, Satan said to God, "Let me at his body and I *guarantee* that he'll curse You."

God gave Satan permission to touch Job physically. The test criterion remained the same—if Job cursed God, Satan would win. If not, God would win. As before, God imposed a restriction: Satan could punish Job's body but he could not take Job's life.

Job writhed in agony. Boils covered his flesh from head to toe. Oozing sores—pain in every cell—it hurt even to breathe. Day after day his body withered away from the physical pain. And then another test. His wife looked upon his miserable state and said, "Why don't you curse God and die?"

Job's faithfulness endured as he replied, "Shall we indeed accept good from God and not accept adversity?" Even through all of this, "Job did not sin *with his lips*"[14] (emphasis ours).

Contest over.

Satan was humiliated once again.

God's glorious sovereignty illuminated the heavenly realm.

Yet things looked very different down below on Job's spot of the earth. Although Job never sinned with his lips, fractures now permeated the foundation of his faith. Job's entire existence had been destroyed—his family, his health, his possessions. He sat in spiritual agony and bewilderment over what his "good God" had allowed to happen.

He began to question God's actions.

As He wrestled with his doubts, three friends arrived to comfort him. Aghast at this human carnage they once had known as "Job," they sat with him in silence for seven days and nights. Their mere presence provided a glimmer of relief for Job that he was not alone in his grief.

But then they spoke.

ROUND 3: JOB'S "FRIENDS" TORMENT JOB.

Eliphaz, Bildad, and Zophar initially came to comfort Job, but their good intentions crumbled into caustic criticisms. *Surely*, they reasoned, *this was the work of an angry God. Job must have greatly offended Him.* They launched a barrage of judgmental criticisms toward Job, claiming that his suffering was a consequence of his own sin.

Eliphaz spoke first, "According to what I have seen, those who plow iniquity and those who sow trouble harvest it."[15]

Bildad followed, "If you are pure and upright, surely now God would rouse Himself for you and restore your righteous estate."[16]

And finally, Zophar chimed in, "If you would direct your heart right and spread out your hand to Him…Then, indeed, you… would be steadfast and not fear."[17]

What could Job do? He was righteous. He could only express bewilderment toward God's actions and try to defend himself against his friends' untrue accusations. Job was already struggling with why God would allow this to happen—he didn't need their criticisms. Job fired back, "For the despairing man there should be kindness from his friend," not accusations.[18] And, "I could say the same things if you were in my place. I could spout off my criticisms against you and shake my head at you. But that's not what I would do. I would speak in a way that helps you. I would try to take away your grief."[19]

Job could bear no more. After all the suffering he'd endured, these false accusations from his "friends" crushed him.

And, *where* was God?

Clearly, even the Almighty had abandoned him. In utter hopelessness, Job fell to a new level of despair. He never cursed God, but now he questioned God's character. Job wanted some answers from the Almighty.

JOB QUESTIONS GOD.

Initially Job assumed that only the wicked suffer, but he also stood convinced that no wickedness dwelt within him. He rationalized that God had erred and was punishing him unjustly. Angrily he demanded that God answer for His actions:

> Do not condemn me. Let me know why You, O God, contend with me. Is it right for You indeed to oppress?...Know then that God has wronged me...I cry, 'Violence!' but I get no answer. I shout for help, but there is no justice.[20]

Job launched into a tirade of accusations against God. His anger turned to bitterness. He *demanded* an encounter with God—even a trial with God to prove his righteousness and demonstrate God's erroneous affliction: "Oh that I knew where I might find Him, that I might come to His seat! I would present my case before Him and fill my mouth with arguments...Let Him weigh me with accurate scales and let God know my integrity."[21]

Job plummeted into a dark, downward spiral; at some point his "blamelessness" turned to sin. He had fallen headfirst into the trap of self-righteousness, even to the point that he elevated himself above

God. He stood tall and proud before the Almighty as he shook his fist in God's face with a final demand: "Oh that God would hear me! Behold, here is my signature; *let the Almighty answer me!*"[22] (Emphasis ours.)

And finally, the Almighty did just that.

GOD QUESTIONS JOB.

God stormed onto the scene in a whirlwind with lightning, a voice of thunder, and a barrage of questions aimed at Job:

> Who is this that darkens my counsel with words without knowledge? Brace yourself like a man; I will question you and *you shall answer me*. Where were you when I laid the earth's foundation? Tell me, if you understand. Who marked off its dimensions? Surely you know! Who shut up the sea behind doors when it burst forth from the womb? Have you ever given orders to the morning or shown the dawn its place? Have the gates of death been shown to you?
> Can you bring forth the constellations in their seasons? Do you know the laws of the heavens?
> Do you know the source of wisdom? Tell me if you are so wise.[23]

(Emphasis ours.)

Each question revealed another aspect of God's supremacy that elevated His sovereign nature to a higher level. And with each question, Job's defiant shoulders sagged lower...and lower...and lower, as the one who demanded a courtroom trial now endured cross-examination by the Judge Himself.

The Almighty continued to question Job. "Have you walked in the crushing depths of the ocean's deepest trench? Do you know the origin of a photon of light? How do you explain lightning?"[24] Midway through His discourse, God paused. By now the humbled Job could barely lift His head. When he did, the Sovereign Ruler of the Universe fired three personal questions that buckled Job's knees (Job 40:2, 8): "Will the faultfinder contend with the Almighty? Let him who reproves God answer it." "Will you really annul My judgment?" "Will you condemn Me that you may be justified?"

Each question addressed Job's specific accusations against the Creator. God offered no explanations, apologies, or regrets for Job's intense suffering. None were necessary. Job's extended suffering had exposed a deep seated and irreverent spirit in the most "blameless and upright man on earth." Job had erroneously believed that his righteousness earned him the right to make demands of a sovereign God.

Job could only bow his head, acknowledge his sin before the Almighty, and proclaim, "Behold, I am insignificant; what can I reply to You? I lay my hand on my mouth. Once I have spoken, and I will not answer; even twice, and I will add nothing more."[25]

Job had arrived at the end of self. In full reverence he proclaimed the grand conclusion that all men who stand before a holy God will someday embrace: "I have declared that which I did not understand, things too wonderful for me, which I did not know...I have heard of You by the hearing of the ear; but *now my eye sees You*; therefore I retract [my accusations] and I repent in dust and ashes"[26] (emphasis ours).

Job had a personal encounter with God; his "eye saw Him." He received an intense knowledge of the Creator that only a few members of the human race ever experience. God immersed Job into His sovereignty, and once we grasp a single thread of sovereignty, all else pales in significance.

THE CONSEQUENCES OF SOVEREIGNTY AND SURRENDER

The book of Job offers many rich insights that can be applied to our lives, but we'd like to focus on three aspects. First, we'll consider this: If God is the Sovereign Ruler of the Universe, can Satan somehow intervene and "snatch away" God's control over our circumstances? Second, we'll address the role that friends play in the life of one who suffers. Finally, we'll consider why God may use the most painful moment in our life to draw us to a deeper level of surrender than we ever imagined possible.

GOD: SOVEREIGN OR NOT

Have you ever felt like God has lost control—that Satan's power must be the source of your turmoil and God is helpless to do anything about it? Over the years I've questioned if Satan could somehow wrestle away God's power here on earth. However, verses like Job 1:11, "Behold, all that he has is in your power, only *do not put forth your hand on him*" (emphasis ours), reveal that Satan may be squarely behind our suffering, but the Master Lapidary remains in rigorous control.

The book of Job makes it abundantly clear: Though Satan has power, God remains in control! *God* initiated the conversation with Satan. *God* granted Satan permission to afflict Job. *God* limited Satan's actions. Few examples in Scripture more clearly display God's sovereignty than His restriction of mankind's arch enemy with two simple spoken words: "Do Not."

WHEN FRIENDS FALL SHORT

"If Jenny had been correctly disciplined there wouldn't be a problem now."

Those words from a dear friend cut deep.

We *had* disciplined Jenny, over and over again—as a young girl and in her current state of rebellion. We grounded her, took away the car and her visitation rights with friends, gave her additional chores, and yet she still snuck out at midnight and disappeared for the weekend.

What else can you do to a seventeen-year-old girl addicted to drugs and to partying?

But our friend's words cut two ways, like a two-edged sword. The words slashed one way, as they wounded us with untrue accusations that we had failed to discipline her, and they cut the other way by reminding us of the times we had judged others for the behavior of their children, errantly thinking as young parents that we had child rearing "all figured out."

The point is this—the pride in our fallen human nature seems to naturally judge another who suffers calamity. It is a grievous error to see someone suffer and to leap to this conclusion: "God must be punishing you."

Such words take a wounded, bleeding soul and painfully grind him against the coarse rasp of guilt and self-condemnation.

And God hates it!

God, through His sovereignty, establishes the conditions, the severity, and the boundaries of our tribulations. He restricts Satan's involvement to a predetermined level. And He assigns a specific task to the friends of those who suffer:

> Now we who are strong ought to bear the weaknesses of those without strength and not just please ourselves. Each of us is to please his neighbor for his good, to his edification.
>
> (Romans 15:1, 2)

> Bear one another's burdens, and thereby fulfill the law of Christ.
>
> (Galatians 6:2)

In the next chapter we'll discuss these passages in more depth, but for the moment let's acknowledge that our responsibility towards the crushed and floundering soul is simple—we are to "bear his burdens and weaknesses." We are to build up the wounded soul, *not* reproach him for "supposed" sin or failure. We *only* rebuke our brothers and sisters for a specific, unrepented sin.[27]

Have wounding words ripped your soul and plunged you to greater depths of darkness? If so, try to understand that such words are often foolishly spoken by one who genuinely desires to help but who is ill-equipped "to comfort as we have been comforted."[28]

Reply with grace to their clumsiness. Pray over them the words of Jesus as He hung on the cross and asked God to forgive them, since they did not know what they were doing. If retribution is required, leave it to God. In the next chapter we'll discover that He has a remarkable way of settling the score.

DOES SOVEREIGNTY DEMAND SURRENDER?

Job experienced a barrage of catastrophes that exceeds our own suffering. Clearly, Job had a mature and solid faith, yet his reverence for God collapsed with intense, extended suffering. Consider his progression:

- Initial impact—Shock, surrender, but a rigid faith that trusted, and even praised, God
- Suffering established—Questions of why God would allow such a thing
- Extended suffering—Questions and doubts about God's character

- Long-term suffering—Anger at God
- "Endless" suffering—Embitterment toward God

Ironically, Job consistently defended his own righteousness before God: "I am innocent." God even confirmed Job's "blameless and upright" nature, but could his nature have been based upon his own strength and performance rather than upon God's empowerment? Was self so radically embedded within Job, as in all of mankind, that he could ultimately condemn God and laugh at His sovereignty while maintaining his own righteousness?

Is that the real purpose behind our crushing trials—to expose and strip away the radical expression of self at its deepest root levels? Is this what's required to lead us to a "radical dependence" upon God?

We believe that every man and woman who has ever experienced extended suffering will eventually question God's character. It's the core expression of "self" in fallen man. We can hide it for a while, but it seems that, at least in those four percent who absolutely surrender, God must reveal it and deal with it.

MY ULTIMATE SURRENDER

I learned a lot about myself, and God, that chilly spring morning in the parking lot. I learned how badly skewed my reasoning about God's character had become. That aspect alone required my repentance and surrender. Hebrews 12:5-7 offered some gentle correction:

> MY SON, DO NOT REGARD LIGHTLY THE DISCIPLINE OF THE LORD, NOR FAINT WHEN YOU ARE REPROVED BY HIM; FOR THOSE WHOM THE LORD LOVES HE DISCIPLINES... It is for discipline that you endure... for what son is there whom his father does not discipline?

I used to equate the phrase "discipline of the Lord" with "punishment by God." Since then, I've learned that the correct Greek definition of the word *discipline* is "training in righteousness." And yet, I've also learned another aspect about suffering that influences discipline. The passage in Hebrews goes on to state:

> Furthermore, we had earthly fathers to discipline us, and *we respected them*; shall we not much rather *be subject* to the Father of spirits, and live?
>
> (Hebrews 12:9, emphasis ours)

My earthly dad would never have tolerated my angry "kicking and screaming" during discipline—it would have been disrespectful. Yet I disrespected the Creator of the Universe with my anger, attitude, and behavior. Like Job, I'd lost my respect of His sovereignty. "Self" was in full rage, and I was far away from "absolute surrender." Still, God kindly and patiently asked, "Do you trust Me?"

Okay, you may be thinking, *I've already fully surrendered to God—so why do the trials persist?*

Dear friend, we ask the following with utmost humility, "Are you sure?"

I learned another aspect about myself that morning—I was *positive* I had fully surrendered and that I had every right to scream my question at God, "Why would you ask me to kill my own child?" His soft reply, **"I asked the same of Abraham. Do you really trust Me? Release her to Me,"** shattered my false illusion like a porcelain plate dropped on a tile floor.

The Father had lovingly and patiently "nailed me."

Deep, deep down in my inner soul I had not released Jenny. I continued to visit her, reach out to her, and think that somehow I could fix her. God's reply hit me like a truck. Thoughts flashed through my mind: *No, I haven't fully surrendered Jenny to You . . . this* is different—she could go to prison and I must "protect" her... She's my little girl, and I refuse to let her go. She needs me. His command to "release her" not only jarred me and left me reeling, it exposed a deeply buried, self-centered, self-protective and independent attitude that shocked and grieved me.

I truly believe that, as I wept in the car those next twenty minutes, I sat at a crossroad in my spiritual life and perhaps Jenny's life as well. I agonized over letting her go. I was humbled and yet terrified of God at the same moment. *Will You send her to prison? What else will You do to Jenny, or to us, if I don't let her go?*

I knew I must surrender *all* to God—every trace of self—and trust Him.

Father, You're correct, I'm still holding on to Jenny. Please forgive me. Lord, I lift her up and release her into Your hands. I trust You to work this out, but I need Your strength. Please help me to truly let go and trust You to care for and protect Jenny.

I took a deep breath, walked into my office, and called the credit card company.

"My daughter is the thief," I told the agent who answered, "and I have no option but to follow through with the prosecution." Thankfully, he detected my dilemma. With an empathetic voice he kindly replied, "We could never ask a dad to do that to his daughter."

Instantly I felt God's sovereignty and love seep into my battered soul. I still feared Him and was sick of the stress and turmoil, but over the next few days I began to sense a relief—that He *was* in control. I had released Jenny into His hands. My only hope was to simply trust Him—that He was able to reach her in ways far beyond what I could imagine.

Four months later Jenny called with this simple request. "I can't live like this any longer. I want to start over with my life. Will you help me?" It was the beginning of her return to God and to us. And

I know from the deepest recesses of my heart that I first had to surrender, trust God, and get out of His way.

Maybe you began reading this chapter angry at God, questioning His very goodness and doubting that He even cares about you. Perhaps you're now pondering if you overstepped your boundary, especially if there's a deeply hidden area in your life that you claim as "yours alone." If so, then have an honest talk with God. Ask for His help to release that "hidden area" and to understand what "radical dependence" means in your life.

On the other hand, if you've made it through this chapter with clenched fists, and you're still so angry at God that you're demanding a "showdown" with Him, then be careful. You just might get it. But before you tie on those boxing gloves, there's another characteristic of God you need to understand and experience. It's in the next chapter. What we've shared here about Job is only part of the story.

Turn the page! What happens next in Job's life exposes the majestic character of God and provides a higher reason for your suffering that just might make every moment of your pain worthwhile.

GEMS 2

PRAYER

Father, I have sinned against You. Please forgive me for doubting Your character. I have condemned You and contended against You. This endless agony has exposed the very roots of my own self-centered nature, and I hate what I see. I repent, Father, and I acknowledge that You alone are the sovereign God. I ask for strength to fully trust You and to absolutely surrender these deep roots of self into Your hands.

Absolute surrender leads to absolute freedom as I learn to absolutely trust God.

Anticipate the following events as you reach the point of absolute surrender:

- You question God's goodness and angrily doubt His motives.
- He exposes an unrecognized flaw from deep within *your* character.
- You acknowledge that He is correct—and you are wrong.
- You recognize that He is sovereign—and, helplessly, that you are not.

CHAPTER 10

Absolute Honor

WE LEFT JOB in our last chapter in a place of unprecedented humility, repentance, and perplexed wonderment. He had come face to face with the Almighty and glimpsed the power and majesty of the Sovereign Ruler of the Universe—and lived. But the encounter undid Job and left him facedown, prostrate in reverent awe of the Almighty.

The story could have ended there but it doesn't. An unexpected twist occurs, a twist that offers infinite hope to every person who has ever suffered unspeakable loss. Intrigued?

Let's pick up where we left off and discover the rest of the story. Again, what follows is based on Scripture, but my (Jim's) imagination fills in the details.

Job slowly lowered himself onto the roughly hewn surface of a wooden plank braced beneath the protective canopy of the aged olive tree. It was the coolest shade available from the searing, midday sun. This had become his spot—his private sanctuary from those who scorned him. His appearance terrified children and appalled the few men and women who wandered by and shook their heads as they spied him, a wretched shell of a man with not even a hint of his former stature. His spot—where years earlier he had gathered olives with his sons. His spot—where he could look across his field that once shimmered with waves of grain almost ready for harvest. His spot—where the mirage from the hot afternoon sun masked the thistles that now grew in defiance of the barley his field once produced.

Everything was different now...unexplainably different...and his mind couldn't rest. God, the immutable, ineffable, and infinite ruler of the stars, had spoken to him and shattered his previously tidy theology.

Why would God choose to display His sovereignty to me, the one who challenged His authority...the one who questioned His character? Why had the Supreme Ruler of the Universe taken time to correct my faulty perspective of Him? I'm but a small speck in the grandeur of creation, and yet the all-powerful and wise Creator singled me out and spoke to me. Why?

Job once viewed himself as a man of wisdom, but now he recognized the truth: He knew nothing...only God had true wisdom. God's plans, God's ways, vastly exceeded the distal limits of his own consciousness.

He forced his restless mind to be still and opened his spirit to pray.

God, what value am I to You? What is my purpose? I've lost my family, my possessions, my health. Everything's gone. My wife loathes me. Men reject me, even my closest friends.

That latter thought stirred deep, jagged memories. His closest friends had judged and betrayed him. Yet after his encounter with God, Job's deep wounds and once-bitter resentment toward them had dwindled. They'd spoken in ignorance, just as he did when he'd challenged the Almighty. *We are all guilty of sin, even in our ignorance.* But they were his closest friends, and the pain of their loss simply added to Job's overwhelming loneliness and abandonment.

His eyes settled on the horizon. A small dust cloud stirred in the distance. *Some poor soul is suffering while traveling in this midday heat,* he mused. Job looked upward into the branches of the olive tree. *The olive tree has life... it serves a purpose in its season... could my season still lie ahead, or did it end with the loss of my children?*

Job glanced eastward again. The cloud had mushroomed in size. As the traveler drew near, it became clear that this was no single person.

Is it three men I see... but what else? Animals... in this heat? What sort of men would be driving poor animals at this time of day?

Job squinted as he peered through the dust and the sun's glare.

He could now make out the form of three men and a pack of animals. Something about the way the men moved seemed familiar. *But who are they, and why are they coming toward my field?*

The men's heads were bowed downward, covered by cloaks for protection from the sun. The animals—seven bulls and seven rams—plodded directly toward Job as they panted, stomped, and whipped their tails to fight away the pestering flies that covered their backs in the searing heat.

As they arrived, Job realized why they seemed familiar. The obvious leader of the three stepped forward and lifted the cloak from over his head.

Eliphaz! His former friend and strongest critic during his intense suffering.

The two had played together as children. They'd worshipped and sacrificed together as young men. As young fathers they'd labored and laughed as they'd worked in the fields to carve out a livelihood for their families. And, as older men, they'd served together as elders in the community.

Oh Eliphaz, you knew me as a brother. How could you condemn me along with the others? How could you reject me...shake your head at me? You ate at my table. We worshipped the same God. Your rejection slashed like a knife in a piercing wound.

Eliphaz slowly raised his face and looked into the eyes of Job.

A thousand emotions rushed through Job. Had Eliphaz come to further condemn him? Why was he here, along with Bildad and Zophar, his other accusers? And why had they come driving fourteen animals?

Eliphaz struggled to speak. Job wasn't sure if his voice cracked because of the dust and the heat or because a strong emotion gripped him.

"Job, I have sinned against you." Tenderness softened Eliphaz's dark brown eyes. "During our last meeting I accused you of sinning against God, but it was I who grievously sinned. God Himself spoke to me, and He condemned me for speaking against you."

Ahh! Job thought. *So Eliphaz, too, has had an encounter with the Almighty. No wonder he speaks in a humble tone!*

Eliphaz reached out and embraced Job in a firm hug. "Job, God honors *you*. He calls *you* His servant. He confirms that *you* speak the truth about Him." Job's throat tightened with emotion as Eliphaz continued. "We," he waved his arm in the direction of Bildad and Zophar, "thought that God only punished the wicked, that He reserved his blessings for the righteous. We now know that both the righteous and the wicked suffer—God alone knows why."

Eliphaz hung his head and whispered softly, "I was wrong, Job. Will you forgive me, my brother?"

Now Job's voice cracked as he struggled to reply, "Of course, my friend."

Eliphaz continued. "There's more, Job. God rejected me, just as I rejected you. He refuses to hear my prayers. He commanded me to take these animals and bring them here for sacrifice."

Finally, the animals made sense.

Eliphaz dropped to his knees on the ground before Job. Bildad and Zophar walked over and knelt beside him. All three looked up at Job, as Eliphaz spoke their unified plea. "God said that you would pray for me—for the three of us—or else He will kindle His wrath against us. Job, you alone can save us from God's hand. Only your righteousness and your prayers can lead us back to the Almighty."

Tears filled Eliphaz's eyes and trickled down his cheeks, making tiny rivers in the brown dust on his face. "Will you pray for us, Job, even though we rejected you and don't deserve it?"

Job's head swirled and the sky seemed to brighten even beyond the midday glare. He closed his eyes and tried to compose himself.

Time stood still. His spirit soared in silent prayer, as God poured out His love into Job's heart and heavenly understanding into his mind! *Praise to You, O Lord! You have revealed my purpose. I live not for myself, but for others, these You have sent to me. My suffering was not in vain; rather, it humbled and refined me like gold. You prepared me to restore my brothers' relationship with You.*"

"Yes, my brothers, I will pray for you," Job finally managed to reply.

Slowly, he arose, opened his eyes, and offered the prayer on their behalf: "Forgive them, O Lord. They did not know what they were doing."

And those words echoed for centuries in the heavenly realm.

Job suffered greatly, and God bestowed upon him the ultimate honor: to save the lives of others.

Only the sovereign God understands why horrible pain is allowed in the lives of those who love Him. But *only* the loving God can use that horrific pain to transform the suffering soul into His fully surrendered servant. Consider this astounding thought by Ravi Zacharias: He states that the primary reason for suffering is to enable a man or woman to serve as a "...redeemer-like figure to those whose lives are devoid of a close walk with God and whose answers may be only surface deep."[1]

Zacharias implies that a higher plane of service exists in God's Kingdom—a service of love in which one is called to intervene on behalf of another. This service requires total dependency upon God, as one takes a stand for the helpless. It often requires self-sacrifice.

When Job prayed for his friends, he became their "redeemer-like figure." You may be thinking, *But Job lost everything for the sake of three friends; is that what God expects of me?* Possibly. But if you read the rest of the story you'll know that God "lifted up" Job's face and restored all his belongings and possessions two-fold.

Let's put aside these blessings for a moment. We believe that God intended something even grander through Job's great suffering than the restoration of his friends, and perhaps Job had a hint as well.

Job makes a phenomenal, prophetic statement during his intense period of suffering. It clarifies our call to suffer for the sake of another. Consider his plea:

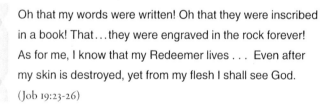

> Oh that my words were written! Oh that they were inscribed in a book! That...they were engraved in the rock forever! As for me, I know that my Redeemer lives... Even after my skin is destroyed, yet from my flesh I shall see God. (Job 19:23-26)

This amazing Scripture records two foundational aspects of Job's great faith: first, his insistence that his suffering was *not* the result of his own sin but the result of a bigger plan that he could not comprehend, and, second, his absolute confidence that God was still God and that someday he'd stand before Him and the mysteries and the pain would dissolve away.

Friend, we've been reading Job's words inscribed in a book, just as he requested! Through God's sovereignty, Job's words, spoken centuries earlier, assure us today that, although our suffering may not make sense, God is God. Our Redeemer lives, and someday we, too, will stand before Him.

Peer into heaven with us for a moment. Imagine the look of surprise on Job's face as he discovers that over three millennia of God's followers would be taught and encouraged by his actions. Job's devotion to God is the ultimate display of honor for a living stone—a gem that sparkles with God's glory and beams messages of hope for centuries to come.

A NOBLE SETTING

The ametrine is finished. All that remains is to mount the stone in a setting for display. I've selected a rectangular pendant for this large and beautiful gemstone.

"Why a pendant?" you might ask.

There are two reasons:

First, the wire frame of the pendant allows maximum light penetration and reflectance. Ametrine is a natural combination of two colored stones; one end is purple and the other end is golden. Mixing between the two colors from the reflected light will occur only in the middle section of the stone.

The second reason is more sentimental. A pendant is worn adjacent to the heart. Jana's birthstone is the golden citrine; Jenny's is the purple amethyst. Our two-tone gem is symbolic of both mother and daughter. Death physically separated Jana from Jenny, but death is temporary. One day mother and daughter will be reunited. This ametrine is a tangible reminder of that future hope.

A God of sovereignty without love would be terrifying. A God of love without sovereignty would be impotent. We have a sovereign, loving God who will work out the best in each of our lives. James R. Chatham (2004)

Our ametrine also represents two aspects of God: His sovereignty and His love. The brilliance of the golden end speaks of God's love for Jana and how His love motivates her to give hope to others in her role as a professional counselor and a servant in ministry. The brilliance of the purple end speaks of God's sovereignty in Jenny's life, as He used her suffering to "save others." I'll share about that in a moment.

Why do sovereignty and love need to be considered together? Because a God of sovereignty without love would be terrifying. A God of love without sovereignty would be impotent. Fortunately we have a sovereign, loving God who works out the best in each of our lives.

Let's consider a few other examples of living stones that God put on display in order to save others.

A NECKLACE OF LIVING STONES

Job must have been shocked when he saw how many people were impacted by the "small story" of his life. We are guessing that you, too, will be shocked when you stand before the Redeemer and discover how many people you impacted through your life.

Do you believe that? Can you imagine that God has something majestic planned for you and others as a result of your ordeal? It's hard, isn't it? But Scripture is filled with testimonies of those who suffered and absolutely surrendered, and later witnessed an eruption of glory. Let's look at four examples:

WOMAN AT THE WELL—DELIVERY OF A COMMUNITY

We've asked this question before but it bears repeating: "Do you believe your life is so badly messed up that God could never use you?" You've suffered greatly and you've surrendered to God, but your life remains in shambles because of past mistakes. You see no hope for the future. Scornful criticism, pain and regret, are your constant companions. If this sounds familiar, you might have traveled the streets of Sychar.

The Jews during Jesus' time despised this city. Their attitude was, "Who could possibly care about Sychar?"

Sychar was a Samaritan village—"a community of dogs," in the opinion of any good-standing Jew. Sychar was also the home of the woman we talked about in Chapter Three—the woman who asked Jesus to give her "living water." In Chapter Three we shared the first part of her story. We said that she was a woman familiar with suffering. She'd had multiple failed marriages, no stable family, no children that we know of, and no hope for a future relationship. The man she currently lived with was not her husband. Her life was in absolute shambles by most cultures' standards.

Now let's consider the rest of her story.

The woman left in haste after speaking with Jesus—so much haste that she abandoned her waterpot at the well.[2] *Who cares about the pot and well water. I've met the Messiah and tasted living water! My heart burns with fire. I know the Messiah. He spoke with me, He cares for me, and He blessed me. I* do *have value, and I have to tell the others!*

"Come, see a man who told me all the things that I have done; this is not the Christ, is it?" The woman's story spread like wildfire among the city. She shared her encounter with everyone she met.[3]

She bore no inhibition, and her words must have carried weight because "from that city many of the Samaritans believed in Him because of the woman who testified."[4] And it didn't end there. The

Samaritans came to meet Jesus, and He stayed with them two days, presumably to teach and heal the sick. The residents of Sychar later proclaimed in reference to this woman:

> It is no longer because of what you said that we believe, for we have heard for ourselves and know that this One is indeed the Savior of the world.
> (John 4:42)

Do you see a pattern? A broken, used, and downcast woman met the Messiah, and, like Job, came face to face with God's sovereignty and love. Her heart exploded, and she rushed back to the helpless in her village as their "redeemer-like figure." And God must have lifted her face...and her reputation.

DANIEL—DELIVERY OF A NATION

Times were dark in Judah but a light burned brightly among the people. His name was Daniel. God bestowed upon him an honor that would stand as a memorial in the history of the Jewish people...and yet, Daniel fulfilled the honor as a captive to a foreign king.

Since a mere youth, Daniel and his nation of Judah had been held as captives in the Babylonian empire, scattered among the former nations. Their captivity had been prophesied for decades because of rebellion against God. Judah worshipped the idols of the surrounding nations. The Lord patiently called them to repent and return. Apparently, God would have honored the righteous prayers of just one man. He later shared in Ezekiel 22:30:

> I searched for a man among them [Judah] *who would...stand in the gap* [a breach in a city's wall] *before Me for the land...but I found no one.*
> (Emphasis ours.)

What a sobering statement. Where were the righteous men and women of that day? Where were those who would repent and return to the one true God? Seventy years *after* Judah's defeat and captivity God found a righteous man, someone to stand in the gap and save others.

Daniel served as a slave to the king. Each day he obediently placed his life on the line for the sake of the king by tasting his food and drink in case they were poisoned. Daniel's confidence in God was legendary. He had been to the lion's den because of his unwavering faith and obedience to God.[5] Daniel had access to God's Word, and he had just discovered in Jeremiah's prophecies that Judah's seventy years of captivity were complete.

But a problem persisted.

God still sought repentance from the nation of Judah. How could a former nation of scattered slaves and beaten captives repent and return to God? There was only one way. Daniel arose early one morning and "stood in the gap" in prayer for his nation:

> Alas, O Lord, the great and awesome God...we have sinned, committed iniquity, acted wickedly and rebelled, even turning aside from Your commandments and ordinances. Moreover, we have not listened to Your servants the prophets...Righteousness belongs to You, O Lord, but to us open shame, as it is this day...O Lord, hear! O Lord, forgive! O Lord, listen and take action! For Your own sake, O my God, do not delay, because Your city and Your people are called by Your name.
> (Daniel 9:4-7, 19)

Daniel's heart-wrenching prayer is one of the most dynamic appeals to God in Scripture. He confessed his sin and his nation's sin. He prayed for God to restore Jerusalem and Israel—not for the people's sake, but for God's sake—for the restoration of His glory.[6] And God immediately responded to Daniel[7] and moved to restore the nation.

It's a repeated theme in Scripture—the righteous interceding before God on behalf of the helpless. It's a theme that resonates unquenchably throughout history. It's the other half of 1 Peter 4:12 and 13 that we left unaddressed in Chapter Eight. The reason we "share in the sufferings of Christ" is to intercede on behalf of others.

We don't claim to fully understand it. It's a heavy responsibility but it's a huge blessing to be used as God's servant and observe His sovereignty and love in action.

Let's consider the ultimate example of One who suffered to save others.

JESUS—DELIVERY OF MANKIND

A titanic clash loomed on this particular night between spiritual darkness and the Source of spiritual light. Jesus stood in bonds, enduring spit, blows to the face, and abandonment by His own disciples. Echoes from a conversation with Nicodemus on a previous dark night (Chapter Two) must have rung in His ears; "…the Son of Man must be lifted up [through crucifixion]; so that whoever believes will in Him have eternal life.[8] …This is the judgment, that the Light has come into the world, and men loved the darkness rather than the Light."[9]

On this particular night darkness would temporarily prevail. Jesus faced the cruellest of deaths—crucifixion by Roman soldiers—and yet, He stood radically surrendered to God and to man, as He fulfilled His role as the sacrificial Lamb of God. Caiaphas, the high priest of the Jews at that time, had prophesied regarding Jesus, "that it is expedient…that one man die for the people, and that the whole nation not perish."[10] The "nation," in reality, referred to all of mankind. He would suffer and die as the true "Redeemer."

Daybreak...blasphemy...a mock trial, and Jesus was delivered to Pilate. In less than three hours the horrible act was completed. Beaten, scourged, and then nailed to wooden beams, Jesus interceded before God as He hung upon the cross. And, as the ultimate example, He surrendered to death on behalf of the entire human race—past, present, and future. Jesus suffered God's wrath for the cumulative sin of this world to restore mankind's relationship with the Almighty.

Perhaps you could imagine suffering on behalf of a community, but for a *nation*, or for *mankind*? Does suffering for the sake of one precious soul sound a little more realistic? Whether it's a nation or one soul, God's infinite love reaches out to save those who seek Him, and His sovereignty cannot be denied. The privilege of serving one or one hundred makes no difference if you happen to be that one who is desperately in need of a "redeemer-like figure."

Let's look at a recent example in which two souls were touched by one servant, specifically prepared by God through suffering.

JENNY—DELIVERY OF TWO DADS

We sat in Jenny's memorial service as vivid memories of her giggles, conversations, and plans flooded our minds and emotionally crushed our spirits.

As I listened, a recent phone conversation played in my mind. "Daddy, I'm so tired of being this way. I hate that I need these pills, and I hate what they do to me. I don't want to live the rest of my life like this."

Jenny's phone call ripped the heart from my chest.

The powerful medications for her severe bipolar disorder were working, yet they created torturous side effects—extreme drowsiness, dry mouth, and a drugged "stupor." She was lonely; she hated the side effects, yet she dreaded where she might return without the pills.

We hung up, and once again I lifted her to God in prayer, but this time my appeal offered no conditions. *Oh, Father, You know how she has suffered and how she continues to do so. There's nothing we can do. Please, Father, be merciful. Please heal her,* or take her home to be with You.

I choked while offering the prayer. In essence, I was requesting God to take her life if that's what He deemed best. I agonized over the appeal. *Such a dangerous prayer! Are you crazy? What kind of a father offers a prayer like that?* Yet I continued to pray daily for Jenny, "Not *my* will, God, but Yours."

Eleven days later Jenny died.

And now as we sat in her memorial service trying to imagine life without Jenny, I felt a huge burden, convinced that my prayer contributed to her death. *It was my fault that she died.*

Encouragement came through several of Jenny's friends, who shared amazing stories of her influence and encouragement in their lives. One even shared that Jenny led her to Christ.

Could this really be true? Our Jenny? We knew she'd changed in the last months of her life. Now we heard evidence from others.

After the service, a man in his fifties approached me. He was crying as if it were *his* daughter who had died. My thoughts ran wild. *Who is this? Why would he be so attached to Jenny? What had been their relationship?*

"Jenny and I met last Thursday at our faith-based, addiction recovery meeting," he explained. "I'd shared about my son who is struggling in a treatment center to recover from severe addictions. I told the group about the tremendous guilt I suffered because he was there and because there was nothing I could do to help him."

He wiped tears from his eye. "After the meeting Jenny came to speak with me. She explained that my son was responsible for his own addictions. She even cared enough to walk me back to my car, and then she said something I'll never forget: 'You can't fight the demons for him, but you can stand beside him while he does.'"

The gentlemen's shoulders shook with sobs. "The moment she spoke those words, I felt released from a huge burden of guilt. I have Jenny to thank for my freedom. I thought she was an angel and now she's dead."

I've replayed that conversation in my mind a million times. Like that gentleman's son, Jenny also fought demons. And likewise, we felt helpless to help her. But the very words that Jenny spoke to encourage that man were the exact words that I also needed to hear. It was as if Jenny was saying to me from beyond the grave, "It's okay, Dad. You stood beside me and did what you had to, and you aren't to blame for my death."

I desperately needed to hear that! We *had* done for Jenny what we could—we'd stood by her. Her death was not my fault, or our fault. God had carefully orchestrated a beautiful sequence:

- Jenny's return to her faith after five years of intense "polishing"
- Jenny's display of God's light as a beautiful gem, as she gave hope to others during the last months of her life
- God's love in taking Jenny from her earthly torment to her new home in heaven
- God's sovereignty and love in bringing Jenny's words back to me through the stranger who reminded me that her death was not my responsibility

And God poured out His love into my heart.

WHO IS GOD CALLING YOU TO "SAVE"?

Are you suffering now? Would it make the agony more bearable to know that God could use your pain to encourage someone else?

What if God said, "If you endure this suffering you'll save someone"? Would you suffer to save a community? A neighborhood? A close friend? How about your child?

The intent of these questions is not philosophical—the intent is to ground your suffering in reality. God can and will use your pain to save others.

Paul said it this way: "Now we who are strong ought to bear the weaknesses of those without strength and not just please ourselves."[11]

At this moment you may be the one with "weaknesses...and without strength" and in search of "one who is strong." But did you consider that at one time the "strong" were also "without strength," as they were being equipped by God? He still prepares His "Jobs" to stand for the helpless.

Are you one of God's selected "Jobs"? Have you ever considered such a thing?

Robert and Michelle never imagined that God would select them either. They were the first couple we knew to experience the loss of a child. Michael, their only child, was brain damaged at birth and lived his short life on a respirator and, all but the last few months, in ICU. They begged and pleaded with God to spare his life as they suffered together, but they maintained their faithfulness and exhibited a solid trust in the sovereign God. They verbally gave Him glory despite their questions.

Many came from Robert and Michelle's workplaces who were not Believers to rally around them. They couldn't understand how a "good God" could allow a child or his parents to endure such suffering, but they couldn't deny this couple's faith. By the end of Michael's eighteen-month life, five people had accepted Jesus Christ as their Lord.

Robert and Michelle often said that what gave them hope and strength was, "knowing that Michael's *little life* had a big purpose."

Author Henri Nouwen says it beautifully: "...when we realize that God has chosen us from all eternity, sent us into the world as the blessed ones, handed us over to suffering, can't we, then, also trust that our *little lives* will multiply themselves and be able to fulfill the needs of countless people?"[12] (Emphasis ours.)

GEMS

PRAYER

Dear Father, I suffer. My pain is intense. But God, I trust You. Please do not leave my agony untended, nor unused. Please, Lord, pour Your love into my heart so that I can love others. And fulfill Your purpose behind my suffering in the lives of those You desire to touch.

God's vast sovereignty governs our pain; His love bestows it for others' gain.

- Job suffered intensely, and three millennia of God's followers have benefitted.

- Consider those you know who may be seeking a "redeemer-like figure" to restore their fractured relationship with God.

- "Standing in the gap" is seldom pleasant, and it may require intensely painful, sacrificial prayer for the sake of another.

CHAPTER 11

A Diamond Named Hope

"Oooh! LOOK, MOMMY! It's beautiful!"
"Oh my, it's as blue as the ocean."
"The bloomin' thing's enormous!"

Whoever comes into the presence of this object of beauty is instantly captivated. This work of art is currently viewed by more people than the Mona Lisa, is of greater value than 100 Lamborghinis, and is about the size of a large walnut. What is it?

The Hope Diamond.

The 45.5 carat diamond of near-perfect clarity is housed at the Smithsonian Institution. Its journey to this place is steeped in legend, intrigue and mystery.

THE JOURNEY OF HOPE

The history of Hope spans centuries, crosses three continents, and passes from the hands of kings to thieves to museums. The earliest historical records indicate that the stone was much larger—about 112 carats. The gargantuan crystal was embedded in the eye of a Hindu goddess idol in the Gorconda region of India. Apparently, someone stole the idol's "eye" and sold it to a French gem merchant, who eventually sold it to King Louis 14th in 1668. The stone was laboriously cut into the famous "French Blue," weighing 67 carats.

It remained in the French Royal Treasury until it was stolen in 1792 during the French Revolution.

In 1812, a beautiful, deep-blue diamond weighing 45.52 carats was presented to a jeweler in London. The Hope Diamond had been recut—*again*.

Over the next 135 years, the stone changed hands and continents multiple times. The diamond was sold to pay private gambling debts and used to raise money for public charities. Eventually it was purchased by gemstone dealer and jeweler Harry Winston, who donated the stone to the Smithsonian in 1958. He mailed it by regular postage—$152 worth—most of which covered insurance for the gem, which is today estimated at $250 million.

During the 1960s, the Hope Diamond was placed in a dark room under an ultraviolet light and studied by scientists. To their surprise, when the light was removed, the stone continued to glow an eerie red for about a minute. It was the first diamond in the world known to exhibit this behavior. Today the glow is the most intense of any blue diamond known.

In 2008, Harry Winston's company decided to commemorate his 50th anniversary donation of the Hope Diamond by contributing an exorbitant necklace setting designed to "show off" the stone. Three designs were prepared, and the public was invited to cast a vote for their favorite setting.[1] The names for the settings were:

- Journey of Hope
- Renewed Hope
- Embracing Hope

These names provide a perfect outline for what we want to talk about in this chapter. We've already explored the "journey of hope," as it relates to history of the Hope Diamond. Now let's focus upon "renewed hope," not in relation to the diamond, but in relation to what God did in us as his "living stones."

RENEWED HOPE

An underlying current sweeps us along in our journey of transformation. When times are dark its presence may seem weak or absent, but it persists nonetheless. It's the current of hope.

JANA'S PERSPECTIVE OF GREEN SAND BEACH

"This is it." I (Jana) pointed to a beach on our map of the Big Island of Hawaii. "This looks like the perfect place to scatter Jenny's ashes."

Jim and I had spent the last five months praying and researching for the ideal location. When she was alive, Jenny had talked often of her desire to go to Hawaii. What we didn't do during her life we would accomplish for her in her death. We agreed: Hawaii was the place... but *where* in Hawaii?

Jim looked at the name beside the tip of my finger. "Hmmm. Green Sand Beach. Intriguing. I wonder if the sand is really green."

"Well, our travel guide says the sand is 'weathered olivine.' Isn't that green?"

"Yep, olivine is also called peridot when it's gem quality," Jim said.

"Perfect. A gemstone beach. Jenny would've loved it," I said wistfully.

Hawaii is the most isolated population center on the face of the earth, with many remote beaches, and our preference was to scatter Jenny's ashes in an isolated area. On the southernmost side of the Big Island, a constant wind blows 27 knots per hour east to west, 24 hours per day, 365 days per year.[2] Beside South Point's jagged cliffs and lava-covered shoreline is a small, remote inlet that includes Papokolea Beach, also called Green Sand Beach. The beach faces the horizon without another land mass for over 2,300 miles. The remote cove is the source of semi-precious peridot that local islanders refer to as The Hawaiian Diamond. The beach is beautiful, but it's not a place to swim, snorkel, or surf because of the strong undertow and sharp lava rocks.

For months, Jim wanted nothing to do with the "precious package" we'd brought with us. Then yesterday, he'd become almost possessive. He brought the box with Jenny's ashes out of the car and placed it in our bedroom.

The next morning our words were few. I gathered towels, camera, a CD player, and about 30 pounds of white coral rock we'd gathered earlier for this occasion and placed everything into a large mesh bag. Jim carried it to the car, along with our "heaviest" load—the five-pound box with Jenny's ashes.

Our friends, Mark and Karen, accompanied us to provide emotional support. As we stepped from the car the view at South Point stole our breath. However, breathing was difficult for other reasons. *Wham!* The wind almost jerked off the car door.

Karen and Mark stayed behind to give us privacy to process the intense emotions that churned inside us. This was a dreaded hike. Our load seemed unbearable. The emotional pain was one kind of weight; the 45-pound mesh bag was another. To carry the bag over the rough terrain we'd have to share the burden. The howling wind made it difficult to hear each other, so we trudged on in silence. Tears streamed down my cheeks, but the sun and wind produced a blast furnace which dried them quickly.

Oh Jenny, I'd give anything to hear your sweet laugh, to look into your eyes and tell you how much I love you, and to snuggle up with you one more time. I sobbed out loud, but Jim didn't hear—the forceful winds masked my wails. I looked at the stern expression on Jim's face. *What are you thinking? I know you're hurting too. I wish we could share our memories of Jenny. This is all too much. Why would a good God allow any parents to carry such a burden?*

I don't know how long the hike took but it felt like a lifetime, as I relived each of her nineteen years of life. With each step I prepared my heart to say this final "goodbye."

We reached an overlook above the cove and the beach and searched for a way down to the water's edge. The clear, azure sky, dark topaz-blue water, and light-green sand beach soothed the eye. The horizon stretched uninterrupted for thousands of miles. I felt conflicted that my eyes could behold such beauty while my heart endured such grief.

In need of a refuge from the harsh wind, I spotted a mini cleft in the rock. I wanted to go sit there, to postpone this event. I pointed to the crevice. Jim nodded, understanding my unspoken intent. My ankle throbbed for attention but the screams from my heart took priority. *I don't want to do this. I don't want to be here. I don't want to let her go.* Our hands, red and sore from the imprint of the bag's handles, mirrored our red eyes, as we both released tears of emotions we'd suppressed for months.

We bent down and crawled into the protective rock. I removed the white coral rocks from the bag. These became our paint brush against the dark black lava. We spelled JENNY, creating a beautiful memorial. A smile crossed my face when I realized the spot we'd chosen to put her name received the last of the sun's daily rays. *Jenny, bathed in final light.*

I didn't want to face what came next.

"One more song. Please let's listen to just one more," I pleaded with Jim.

"It's time," he said. Jim picked up the box, opened it, and carefully slid the sealed, clear plastic bag into his hand. "You stay here. It's too dangerous for you to climb down these jagged rocks with your ankle."

Perched on a large rock, I watched, as Jim climbed down to the water's edge. He looked back up at me and nodded. Holding the bottom of the plastic bag, he raised his arm high, and in one swift motion Jenny's ashes became airborne. *Swoosh*! A gust of wind snatched the cloud of ash upwards and then swirled around to encircle Jim. The wind whipped around once more, and suddenly the ashes vanished. Nothing remained. "A vapor in the wind, a wave tossed in the ocean,"[3] ashes to the sea. Jim climbed back up and joined me on my perch. Tenderly he looked into my eyes.

"Did you see that?" Jim asked.

"I did." I said, choking back tears.

"It's finished." Jim said. "We did it." He wrapped his strong arms around me in a tender embrace. In that moment I no longer noticed the harsh wind, sun, or heat—all my senses were tuned into Jim—the steady *thump* of his heart and the strength I gained from his strong arms. The last few months had been a dry desert of hopelessness, but in that moment a tiny trickle of hope flowed through me, hope that maybe better tomorrows lie ahead. For today, that was enough.

JIM'S PERSPECTIVE OF GREEN SAND BEACH

We stood at the trailhead and surveyed the path that led to Green Sand Beach. Two words came to mind as I considered the two-mile trek that lay ahead: *brutally harsh*. The black, jagged rocks would rip and tear any flesh that stumbled and fell upon them. Through my "geologist eyes" the hardened lava looked as if it had violently exploded from the nearby crater and cooled only yesterday, forming an abrasive, glassy-sharp surface. *What a harsh setting*, I thought... *the vicious heat and chaos that formed this place mirror my own emotions and the turmoil that surely lies ahead.*

"I'll carry the bag," I told Jana.

"I can help!" she instantly replied.

"Nope, I've got it," I insisted, "just watch your step on these sharp rocks." I felt protective of Jana—I wanted her to focus on her footing with her sore ankle, rather than assisting with the bulky bag. And it would grant me the honor of serving Jenny one final time.

As we stepped onto the trail and into a blast furnace of heat, wind, and emotional furor, two cataclysmic forces ripped at my heart. First, there was the agony of releasing Jenny's ashes. They were our last, tangible remnants of her. I felt connected to her through those ashes. I sensed her presence when I approached the box—I could almost see her, touch her. To scatter and throw away the ashes was to throw *her* away! I questioned if I could do it.

Second, there was the agony of *not* releasing her ashes. Intellectually I knew the ashes weren't Jenny—they contained nothing of her spirit or soul. And, as her father, I knew Jenny would want me to dispose of them—she wouldn't have wanted that pressure on Jana. We both needed closure to her death. Scattering her ashes would give us the closure we needed. The two contradicting emotions... *don't throw her away,* and conversely, *let her go*... collided within me like waves in the ocean and intensified with each step of the journey.

Several minutes into the hike, my arms ached, as my fingers strained to grasp the hard plastic handles of the heavy bag, but the physical burden was nothing compared to the emotional weight that crushed my heart. *We shouldn't be here, shouldn't be doing this... no parent should,* I told myself as I changed hands more and more frequently.

"Okay, let me help with the bag!" Jana insisted.

Begrudgingly, I gave her one handle, and, for the first time in years, instead of being on polar opposites about how to "manage" Jenny, we shared the burden in quiet agreement.

We leaned into the hot wind and pressed onward. Nineteen years of conversations with Jenny flooded my mind, forming a chronology of her life. Her own words spoke an epitaph which roared louder in my soul than the rushing wind in my ears:

"*Daddy, I love you, I love you, I love you!*" Jenny, at two years old, was affectionate and precocious. After the "umpteenth" warning to be quiet during church service, I picked up my lacy-dressed daughter and carried her down the center aisle towards the exit. She knew the discipline that was coming, and she grabbed my face with both hands, looked into my eyes, and loudly spoke those words while the congregation laughed.

"*Daddy, let's jump on the trampoline—with Rudy.*" Eight years old, Jenny was fun-loving and creative. Golden retrievers are calm, loyal, and patient—but they stress when airborne. Rudy had his first encounter with weightlessness after only three synchronized jumps between Jenny and me. We burst into laughter as he attempted to run in midair, but we immediately stopped and consoled him as we recognized his panic.

"*I was skating down the hill while Rudy pulled me, and then Mom whistled for Rudy.*" Jenny in middle school—reckless and adventurous. She'd gripped Rudy's leash, as he'd trotted down the bike trail toward home, the wheels of her new inline skates turning faster and faster. Jana, unaware of Jenny's "thrill ride," whistled for Rudy, who immediately shifted gears from "trot" to "full sprint." Jenny crashed and broke her wrist.

"*Come on, Jessie. Jump! It's only water.*" Courageous and encouraging, Jenny spoke these words to her best friend, as the two eighth-graders tried out for the dive team. It was Jessie's first time on the high-dive platform. Jenny had backflipped off the platform just a few minutes earlier. Now, through her words and example, she imparted confidence to Jessie as she nervously studied the long drop to the water below. Jessie stood for 45 minutes on the platform until she finally embraced Jenny's assurance: "You can do it." Jessie made the plunge—and the dive team.

"*Daddy,* I am *driving slowly!*" "Stubborn" and "defiant" described our teenager. Her words had come just three seconds before sliding sideways down a long Alaska hill into eight other cars that had also lost control on the icy highway.

During the last five years of her life, all kinds of "wrecks" swirled around Jenny. The stress of cleaning up her messes created an emotional chasm between Jana and me. Five miserably hard years for the three of us—and to end like this. I glanced sideways and watched a tear evaporate from Jana's cheek. *What thoughts are tearing at your heart, Honey?* I couldn't ask—the howling wind made conversation impossible. I gripped the bag's handle securely and imagined it was Jana's hand.

"No, I'm not doing drugs!" A drug test hours after her denial confirmed that our eighteen-year-old had, once again, lied. This denial joined a list of other falsehoods—she'd been untruthful about her actions concerning bulimia, sex, and popping pills. But this lie was different. It led to a second inpatient treatment center and successful stabilization of her bipolar disorder, which would place her on the road to recovery.

"I'm so lonely. Can I come to Alaska and visit you and Mom?" Jenny, a week before her death—relational and reaching out for help. On previous visits she'd fallen back into unhealthy habits with old friends. We knew it was best to visit her in Texas. I told her, "No, not now," but I reminded her that I had a trip scheduled to see her in just two weeks. Then she died.

I wasn't there when she needed me most. She died alone, and lonely. *Oh Sweetie, I miss you so much! I'd love to hear you giggle once again. I never want to let you go, and yet, I* have *to let you go.* The bag was so heavy. *Please, Father, give me the strength to do this.*

We finally arrived at the cove with its steep, rugged walls. The pounding surf reflected my inner turmoil. We made it down to an overhanging ledge on the far side of the cove. Jana, with amazing forethought, had prepared a private memorial ceremony for the two of us. We prayed over Jenny's ashes and acknowledged her release into the Father's hands. We listened to the song, *I Can Only Imagine,* which speaks of that joy we will feel when we meet Jesus in heaven.

We ached together over Jenny's absence, but we also took courage in knowing that one day we'd see her again.

Jana wanted to listen to one more song, but I couldn't. The few moments in the refuge of the rocks away from the harsh wind and sun had revived me. Our words of reflection upon Jenny's life had drawn me back to the stark reality that she was gone and to the purpose of this trek. During our prayer time God had risen up within me a forceful resolve to finish the task before us.

"It's time," I said. We removed the plastic bag with her ashes from the box, and I carefully climbed down the steep wall. Because of her fragile ankle, Jana remained behind, standing on a boulder where she could watch.

A flat rock near the upper reaches of the swelling surf...this will work.

I stepped down near the rock, opened the plastic bag and grabbed its base. I timed the ocean surges with the persistent easterly wind. At just the right moment, I stepped out on the far edge of the rock, flung the bag outward while holding its base, and watched her ashes swirl upward and over the water. Suddenly the east wind swirled westward, and a cloud of "Jenny" dusted my hair, face, eyes, and arms with remnants of her. It was as if she comforted me with one final embrace, one last kiss "goodbye."

Immediately, a huge burden lifted from my shoulders and my soul. An overwhelming peace flooded my soul—a peace that could only come from God. Jenny was free, but *I was the one* who had been released. I stood on the rock, watching her ashes rapidly disappear in the blue water, as surges rushed over the rock and soaked my shoes. It was the strangest feeling, almost one of elation—we *both* were free.

After a few minutes I climbed up the rocks to where Jana stood and put my arms around her. "We did it," I said. It was a comforting feeling—saying the word "we"—another release. As a couple, we'd broken through a barrier. For the first time in years we'd labored together to complete a task focused upon Jenny. We'd taken the first steps back towards one another in our relationship.

We climbed the steep slope hand in hand. We faced an immediate struggle, as we began our return trek across the rough volcanic terrain to reach the Jeep, but, as with future battles, we'd do so hand in hand. And God would bless us by renewing our hope. Green Sand Beach had provided us with two things we desperately needed: an ending…and a new beginning.

EMBRACING HOPE

God ignited a spark of hope in both Jana and me that afternoon at Green Sand Beach. Even though we'd begun our hike on very different emotional pathways, our paths converged at the secluded cove where we'd scattered Jenny's ashes. We returned in unity birthed by God through hope. Hope, in fact, *only* comes from God.[4] Consider these quotes:

- "God is the only one who can make the valley of trouble a door of hope." Catherine Marshall[5]
- "Would you allow suffering to lead you to the very heart of God, a place where you can find the comfort and peace that you crave as well as the hope that has the power to transform your tomorrows?" Nancy Guthrie[6]
- "The hope that the Bible speaks of is no empty wish or attempt at positive thinking. Who—not what—we put our hope in is what makes all the difference." Patricia Raybon[7]

Hope rests upon the stable foundation that God is still God, no matter what. He is sovereign, He is loving, and He will never change.[8] Hope leads us toward intimacy with God. "That is always God's purpose (intimacy with Him): to use whatever means He sees fit to bring us to a closer relationship with Him, to create in us a faith that will give us the strength to keep holding on to hope...that what is unseen will be seen."⁹

Hope is progressive. It's a series of *simple* steps, not a grandiose conclusion that you jump to overnight. It begins with the validation of our pain and ends with our display of God's glory as we praise Him and give hope to another. This is the reason we wrote this book—to *share our hope* with you and to *embrace hope together.*

The progression of HOPE begins with emotional hopelessness. It advances through a rational thinking process that leads to a behavior shift. It climaxes with a complete lifestyle change—a God-centered hope. We'll use the acronym **H.O.P.E.** to display the four distinct steps.

    H—Hear and validate the pain
    O—Observe an ending to pain
    P—Persevere through pain
    E—Eternal focus beyond pain

As a couple, we each experienced hope differently—in different ways and at different times. It's important to realize that what gives one person hope may not necessarily be what gives another person hope. As you work through the acronym, we pray that the progression will be clear to you and that you'll see the different ways hope manifests itself.

H—*Hear and validate the pain.* Hopelessness thrives when a wounded soul feels isolated, ignored, or misunderstood. Rod Wilson writes in his book *How Do I Help a Hurting Friend:* "When people are in the midst of grief, particularly the early stages, they do not need biblical exegesis or systematic theology. What they need is the presence of Christ and the work of the Holy Spirit demonstrated through our presence."¹⁰ When a person is in a hopeless state, one of the most loving things you can do is to listen and reflect their feelings and validate their pain.[11] Phrases like, "You are really hurting..." or "You seem to be grieving about..." and "You sound completely discouraged..." acknowledges an individual's personal expression of pain. Hope often cannot move forward until pain is acknowledged.[12] Scripture tells us to "weep with those who weep." Jesus did this. Upon witnessing Mary and Martha's agony after their brother's death, Jesus' response is recorded with two short words, "Jesus wept" (John 11:35). He heard and validated.

> ***Jim:*** I hit one of the lowest points of my life the fourth day following Jenny's death. I'd had a hard conversation with Jenny regarding her finances only a week earlier. It was my last conversation with her. I poured out my agony and my regret over the conversation to Jim Carroll, a dear friend who'd traveled down from Alaska to Texas to support me. He listened for probably fifteen minutes, eye-to-eye, without interrupting and with nods of affirmation. Then I lamented, "How insensitive I must have been... If only I'd known she would die four days later... I pressed her unnecessarily." Then Jim spoke these powerful words: "You know that's a lie from the devil—you could never have known this would happen. You spoke correctly to Jenny." With those simple words, he validated my pain and exposed the enemy's deception. This birthed hope within me.
>
> ***Jana:*** Unlike Jim, I had a hard time verbally sharing my pain with other people—yet I yearned for someone to listen. I discovered the safest way to express my agony was to write. I poured out my heart during the middle of many sleepless nights through long e-mails to a couple of dear friends. Their tender responses validated and encouraged me to keep

writing. Their willingness to protect my vulnerability and provide a safe place for me to wail through the keyboard sparked my first glimpse of hope.

O—*Observe an ending to pain.* Hopelessness is fueled by desperation when no end is in sight. First Peter 5:10 says, "And after you have suffered *for a little while…* God *…will Himself* perfect, confirm, strengthen, and establish you," (emphasis ours). Did you see that? *God Himself will* intervene after our suffering has lasted for a little while. The duration of our suffering is carefully monitored by the Father and, apparently, its termination is too important to be assigned to God's messengers, the angels. God Himself delivers us! You may believe the fiery, crushing pain can never end, but God promises *that it will*!

> **Jim**: *Father—I can't bear the thought that Jenny may have died alone or that Your hand wasn't with her to the very end. Were You with her? Please show me!* That was my cry the day we learned of her death. I couldn't bear the thought of living with such uncertainty, without knowing if she was cared for during her final days and hours. Over the next six days, the Lord provided 21 examples of His presence with her up to the very last moment. I know, because I recorded each one—from handwritten Scriptures in her wallet, to a perfectly cleaned and prepared apartment, to specific testimonies of friends. God comforted me when He spoke to my heart, **Her death didn't take Me by surprise.** Different levels of pain exist. Although the intense ache of missing Jenny did not subside for many years, the "fiery pain" that I experienced after we received the news of her death lessened, as I received these confirmations that God's hand had indeed hovered over the final hours of her life.

Jana: For years I couldn't comprehend how or if the intense pain could ever end, and then I became afraid that it would. I didn't want to stop hurting because I was afraid I'd forget her. My distorted rationale was that as long as I hurt I would remember and stay connected to my daughter. I asked others who had experienced similar losses and discovered I was not alone in this type of irrational thinking. About three years after Jenny's death, we were asked to share our testimony at church during a sermon series on the book of Job. We opened and ended our story with Job 1:21: "...The LORD gave and the LORD has taken away. Blessed be the name of the LORD" (emphasis ours). As we spoke those words, we thought of Jenny, whom the Lord had taken, but behind us on the large projection screen was a picture of Jim and me holding our newborn granddaughter, a reminder of how life goes on and that the Lord also gives. Looking at the precious face of my granddaughter was a "marker"—a moment in time in which the joy of being part of her life filled me and eased the pain of losing my own daughter. For the first time since Jenny's death, I felt hope for the future. I had much to live for.

P—*Persevere in pain.* Perseverance is not a pleasant phase in the progression of hope. It's like the daily grind of the gemstone—some days we just have to grit our teeth and keep pressing forward. Scripture tells us that we are to rejoice in the daily grind because this is the phase in which God accomplishes character in our lives. "We also exult in our tribulations [suffering], knowing that tribulation brings about perseverance; and perseverance, proven character; and proven character, hope..." (Romans 5:3-5). The goal is that we exhibit "proven character"—the solid confidence that we will survive and that God will somehow take care of the remaining issues.

Jim: In the years following Jenny's death I was able to persevere by discovering a way to enjoy life and laughter again. After two years away, our daughter Julie and her husband returned to the area. Julie and I began a new hobby of hunting, harvesting, and preserving salmonberries, currants and other natural fruits and berries in Alaska. These intentional activities took my mind away from the endless playbacks of what we might have done differently with Jenny. Instead, I learned to trust that God's sovereignty prevailed during the final days of her life—and it changed my character. Jana will confirm that I'm a different person today. I'm much more accepting of those things I can't explain or change. I'm more at peace with myself—and with God.

Jana*:* Months after Jenny's death I began physical therapy for my ankle and shoulder, which included a swimming regimen. I have a love/hate relationship with swimming. I love to push myself to the point where the only thing I can think about is lifting one arm and then another. Numb, I take a deep breath, consider my goal of three more laps, and push on. When I *feel the pain of physical exhaustion,* all I have to do is stand up, catch my breath and go on—a behavioral change. I learned to persevere through emotional distress in much the same way. After Jenny's death, I frequently felt emotionally "numb." I persevered through emotional exhaustion by pushing myself over and over to do the "next thing." When I felt I couldn't go on, I stood up and took a deep breath—a behavioral change. I stopped thrashing around in my ruminating thoughts and high energy activities as I "stilled" myself physically, emotionally, and spiritually. I sat quietly, prayed, and listened to God. *I allowed myself to feel the pain.* Then I did a quick self-inventory to discover any unchecked emotions and bodily sensations, such as tightness or uneasiness. I considered if my negative self-talk had become louder than my positive self-talk. I made myself "throw away" negative thoughts and chose instead to think on what was true, honorable, just, pure, lovely, commendable, excellent, and worthy of praise.[13] Continually making that choice changed my behaviors and my character. Now, instead of avoiding quiet time with God, I pursue quiet times where I can be intimate with Him.

E—*Eternal focus beyond pain.* The essence of "E"—eternal focus—is realized when God "lifts our face." This phrase comes from Job 42:8 and 9, which says that the LORD accepted Job and literally means God *lifted his face.* At that moment, Job's eyes shifted from an internal focus to a Divine, external focus.

Imagine God, reaching down with His hand from heaven and gently touching your chin. He tenderly lifts your downcast face upward...toward the heavens...toward Him. He invites you to look into His eyes. You dare to do so, and then He smiles with fatherly affection. Divine love, confirmation, and approval flood your soul. This description may sound a bit ethereal, but the idea is rooted in Scripture. When God lifts our face to Him, what do we experience?

- Peace and security fill our being (Isaiah 26:3).
- Our vision shifts from self to God (Ps. 25:4, 5).
- We focus on what is eternal rather than what is temporary (2 Cor. 4:16-18).
- We praise and love God in our current circumstances (2 Cor. 12:8-10).
- We display His glory (2 Cor. 3:18).

- We become aware of God's higher purposes (Isaiah 55:8, 9).
- We reach out to nourish and love others in need (John 13:34, 35; 2 Cor. 1:3-5).

These changes are only possible because we've been restored to the image of Christ to reflect His glory. Put simply, the source of our eternal hope is God Himself through His love. Hope's basis is love, administered to our hearts through the Holy Spirit.[14] We now have a God-centered hope, and our natural response is to reach out and encourage others.

> **Jim:** Because Jenny had rebelled against God and our parental authority in her teen years, I questioned if heaven was her spiritual destination. The uncertainty of this tormented me. Then, after Jenny's memorial service, I met the man who said that Jenny had changed his life and had been "an angel" to him. Jenny had given hope to that man—and in that moment God gave hope to me *by lifting my face.* It was as if God gently tilted my chin, smiled into my eyes, and said to me, ***Do you see how I changed her and used her for good?*** Peace, joy, and praise exploded in my heart. I saw God's higher purposes in Jenny's life, in that man's life, and in my life. A desire for heaven swelled within my spirit, as did a desire to assure others in crises that God's love would prevail. That desire became so strong that it contributed to the birth of this book.
>
> **Jana:** The week after we scattered Jenny's ashes, Karen and I went to Maui for her birthday, without our husbands. We anticipated a fun-filled week. However, I became downcast, as my underlying inability to trust others had

now collided with my ability to trust God. I shared my fears with Karen. We prayed, poured over Scriptures, and she handed me the book that she was reading, *Trusting God, Even When Life Hurts,* by Jerry Bridges. That week, while sunbathing, I soaked in God's warmth, and His love flooded the crevasses of my soul. While I was sitting under a palm tree, God reached down and lifted my face towards Him. He helped me see a higher purpose for my pain—that He could use my pain to encourage others. The intensity of His love consumed me to the point I *had* to share with others my discovery. After returning home, I taught two different classes over the next few weeks. One class was based upon Bridges' book. I co-led the other class with a widow, and we used the book *Shattered Dreams,* by Larry Crabb. At the end of the class one member accepted Jesus Christ as her Lord and Savior. God had indeed lifted my face, and the hope with which He had filled me naturally flowed over to others. I began to minister to people in prison. I worked with addicts, those who love addicts, and trauma survivors. Ultimately I went to graduate school and became a professional therapist.

As a therapist, I've presented the H.O.P.E. acronym to several clients. One client who suffered multiple, horrific abuses and ultimately abandonment said, "Jana, this acronym is so helpful. I can see that I've moved past the letter 'H'—You heard and validated my pain. I've also moved beyond the 'O'—I've observed an ending to some of my pain by making new friends and learning to trust again. I realize now I'm on the letter 'P'—I need to persevere. It helps when I have a really down day to remind myself of my progress and that things won't be this way forever. One day I'll get to the 'E' and God will use my pain to help others."

I know my clients are at the 'E' when they recognize their trials may not have been entirely about them, and they gratefully anticipate helping another. Norman Wright reports that a trauma survivor knows they are getting better and recovering when they "discover a new and deeper sense of empathy for the wounded around them. A trauma survivor can actually become a wounded healer and have a greater compassion for others."[15]

I often suggest my clients try to imagine themselves as a kaleidoscope. The broken and shattered pieces inside the scope represent their life stories. I put my hand under my chin and slightly lift it and say, *"To reveal the greater beauty of brokenness the pieces must be lifted up to the light."* They may not understand at first how God can use each sharp edge of abuse, every little fracture of grief, and every splinter of hopelessness to reflect His glorious light and to form a beautiful design. But over time my goal is to help them see God's plan and how He creates beauty from brokenness with His light. That's who I am...I'm a hope giver. I don't fix brokenness; I only help change their perspective. I lift their life up to God's light. I help them see the bigger picture of how the pieces create beauty. I share the progression of H.O.P.E.

One client looked up at me through tears, after sharing her shame and guilt of suicidal thoughts, and said, "How can you have hope for me? Your life seems perfect. I bet you've never experienced hopelessness."

I smile.

I know.

I'm a screaming stone.

GEMS 2

PRAYER:

I pray that God, the source of hope, will fill you completely with joy and peace because you trust in him. Then you will overflow with confident hope through the power of the Holy Spirit (Romans 15:13, NLT, emphasis ours).

Hope is progressive; although it is future focused, it is lived out in the present.

- ♦ Hope comes from God.
- ♦ Hope rests upon the stable foundation that God is still God, no matter what.
- ♦ Hope is a uniquely personal journey.

Epilogue

Ten years have passed since our early morning scream. Since that dark morning, our journey has been one of spiritual growth and intense transformation. We've walked through the H.O.P.E. process, and today our passion is to encourage others who desperately need hope.

This book is an expression of our desire to lift the face of the downcast. We yearn to walk beside others afflicted by trauma, such as childhood abuse, divorce, or death of a loved one. We desire to reach out to parents or family members who have a loved one who suffers with a mental disorder—to remind them that they are not alone. We long to help those in pain recognize that there is a God who loves them—a sovereign God who has their best interest at heart and who created them for noble purposes.

We've learned that one facet of grief is that anniversaries and other significant dates often evoke intense emotions. We encourage those who struggle with such dates to create new, positive memories.

Jim and I scheduled a trip to the Oregon coast with friends with the intention of creating new memories. I (Jana) went to the beach late in the evening on Jenny's birthday. I carried a bouquet of 24 long-stemmed red roses—19 to represent each year of her life and five to represent the number of years since we'd last hugged her. My thought was to scatter the petals along the beach, as I reflected on each year of life since her birth. As I walked and scattered the petals, a humorous memory popped into my mind. In preparing for Julie's wedding, Jenny had often joked, "This is really nice, but my wedding's gonna cost you more!" At that moment I realized that I had become Jenny's flower girl. Jenny was now in heaven with her heavenly Groom. Indeed, her wedding *had* cost us so much more. For Jim and me, the price was her absence from our lives. But the cost for Christ was even greater—He had given His life for His bride. The following morning, I penned these words:

MY DAUGHTER'S FLOWER GIRL
By Jana Chatham
February 2009

A rose for each year of life,
Plus the weight of five.
Embrace the long stems, cuddle her again.
It felt good to "hold" her in my arms.

Rose one caused a smile, remembering her first—
A year of discovery, giggles, and laughter.
The petals, soft and warm in my hands,
Their fragrance filled my senses of her infant innocence.

The second, just as sweet,
Holding it next to my cheek.
I laughed out loud and thought of her not so little voice
Full of life and energy, none could compete.

Third, fourth, and fifth passed through fingers quickly.
A toddler transforms, a little girl is "born."
Discovering and developing her own identity.
Reliving, this flower girl mourns.

Sixth, seventh, eighth, and ninth prompted rhythmic steps back in time.
Direction and focus changed.
Interrupted by things in the distance,
Allowed outside distractions of years to consume.

Tenth, eleventh, and twelfth, adolescence snuck up...
The changing tide requires attention.
Run, never turn your back,
Constantly aware of the unstoppable.

Teenager, a joy and a challenge.
Remember the good; it was there,
Her silly things, pranks and jokes.
The fragrance is strong but falls to the wave.

Fourteenth, fifteenth, sixteenth and independence is near.
The power of a car, new friends and a phone.
Surge from a wave. Step faster. Be alert!
Tenderly and intentional drop one, two, and then three.

Ouch! The seventeenth pierced more than skin.
Thorns, some intentionally ignored.
It's a risk we take when close enough to feel.
Experience the splendor, their absolute being.

Eighteenth. Dark. Missing petals.
Held close, still soft,
Even when bruised a beautiful rose remains.
Slowly, one by one, petals fall from my hand.

Nineteenth bud clung to the stem.
The only rose to feel cold against my skin.
Hold tight to "the bouquet." No I won't let go!
A petal tissue wiped away the tears, O Lord, not again!

Walking along I comprehend,
I am and was "My Daughter's Flower Girl."
Her wedding cost me more than most.
The Groom picked up the tab, He paid it *all*.

Holding the long, cold stem in hand
His gift for only a little while.
He whispers now and forever, "She's with me."
With all of my might I throw it to the deep.

The final four feel cold to my touch.
Their fragrance always the same,
Whether lovingly held or crushed in pain.
Only a memory of days once known.

A single rose remains.
Another year gone.
I glance back from where I've come,
Petals dropped one by one.

Twenty-four roses to remember my child.
The tide retreats, I rush to beat the waves—
Which return as I stake the final one.
In a sprint I cry... it is done.

A rose for each year of life,
Plus the weight of five.
I am and was "My Daughter's Flower Girl,"
Along the beach dropping petals one by one.

In loving memory of Jenny Lynn Chatham.
February 16, 1985 – July 5, 2004

EPILOGUE

The day after I scattered the petals, we left before dawn to fly back to Alaska. My dear friend went for a walk that morning, and, after seeing the string of petals I'd scattered the evening before, wrote the following:

DEVOTION BY A FRIEND

Rose petals the color of a bleeding heart washed ashore today.
As if by a grieving mother struggling to shed the cocoon of sorrow,
The petals lay one at a time in a trail of tears and thankfulness
Outlining the shore.

The rose petal residue, like the memories they represent,
Decorates the beach on this sunny, blue day—
A bright contrast to the gray sand.

A small child picks up the petals
And places them one by one in her mother's hand.
Carefully they inspect the deposit of crimson treasure.
Mother and daughter are sparkling in the sun today.
They do not know this is a necklace of devotion
Unstrung and given back to the Creator in an act of gratitude and grief.

Rose petals the color of a bleeding heart washed ashore today,
Leaving a trail of discovery and joy,
The cost of which could never be counted.

Chapter Questions

The following questions are designed to take you deeper into the messages in each chapter. Use them for personal reflection and journaling or as part of a group discussion. We recognize that some readers will be at different stages in their journey. Some may be at the beginning of their scream and in desperate need of comfort. Others may feel "stuck" in the monotonous daily grind and could use a dose of inspiration. Still others are near the end of a long period of grief, and they now feel ready to embrace a new perspective that includes helping others. We encourage you to choose those questions that speak to you in your personal journey. The first few questions in each chapter are designed for personal reflection and prayer; the latter focus on a deeper study of the Scriptures.

CHAPTER 1

1. Are you currently a "screaming stone"? Jana shared that during her greatest points of grief she felt "isolated" and "surrounded by darkness." Darkness can be dangerous. Pray. Turn on *physical* lights and saturate yourself with *spiritual* light by reading God's Word.

2. In intense emotional pain we often desire numbness, isolation, or a "quick fix." Who or what have you turned to in your darkest hour (for example, people, food, drugs, busyness, or alcohol)? Have you ever turned to God and His Word? If so, describe what you noticed.

3. Become aware this week of how God brings light into your darkness, even if it's only a small flicker of encouragement. Journal your thoughts and responses to your awareness of His light.

4. Reflect on Isaiah 60:1-3; 2 Samuel 22:29; Psalm 18:28; and Psalm 119:130. What does God do with your darkness?

5. Read Psalm 18:1-6, 46-50. Describe how David saw himself and his relationship with God. How did David turn his scream of pain into a cry of praise?

6. What associations does Peter make when he refers to us as "living stones" (1 Peter 2:4-10)? Why do you think God refers to Himself as "the Rock" (Isaiah 26:4) and to Jesus as "the cornerstone" (Ephesians 2:20, 21)? Read Psalm 118:22; Isaiah 8:14; and Isaiah 28:16. What special understanding would the Israelites have had about stones that may be less familiar to us in our modern, Western culture? Why do you think stones were used as monuments to mark what God did in the lives of His people? How could you, as a living stone, serve as God's monument to others?

7. Who encouraged you when you were a "screaming stone"? What did they do? Write a note of thanks to one of your encouragers.

8. Do you know someone who is currently a "screaming stone"? Ask God to show you something you can do or say to encourage this person.

CHAPTER 2

1. What are your childhood wounds? How did each fracture contribute to your personality today?

2. Have you ever felt the presence or perceived the influence of "evil spirits"? What were the circumstances? Can you identify negative emotions, such as fear or anger, which happened as a result of this encounter? Consider if any of your current attitudes or behaviors are rooted in this situation.

3. Do you have behaviors that were necessary for survival as a child that are no longer healthy as an adult? Read Luke 10:38-42. When Jesus visited the home of Mary and Martha, the two sisters behaved differently. What childhood factors do you think might have prompted their different behaviors? Which behavior did Jesus praise?

4. Read Isaiah 43:18, 19. What instruction does this verse offer in light of your emotional or spiritual wounds? What hope does this verse offer? What "new thing" is happening in your life that may help heal your old wounds? Read 1 Kings 17; 2 Kings 19:1-36; and 2 Kings 20:1-6. How did God rescue His people from evil or pain?

CHAPTER 3

1. We equate the "glowing stone" with a person who acknowledges God and yearns for relationship with Him. Would you describe yourself as a "glowing stone"? Have you acknowledged the existence of God? What drew you to Him?

2. Who do you know that is a "glowing stone"—someone who is passionate about God? What qualities do they exhibit that you admire?

3. When do you like to meet with God—in the privacy of darkness, like Nicodemus; in midday public gatherings, like the woman at the well who told others about Jesus; or at some other time?

4. Read Psalm 42:1 and 2. Notice all the action words in this verse. Can you identify with these powerful verbs? What does the Psalmist ask in verse 2?

5. Look up the word "light" in a Bible concordance. Jesus calls Himself the light of the world (John 8:12). What do you think He meant by this statement? What are the qualities of light? How did Jesus exhibit these?

6. Jesus says, "...you are the light of the world" (Matthew 5:14). Name two ways you are a light to others. What is the connection between your light and Jesus' light?

CHAPTER 4

1. The birthmark of misplaced faith happens when we place our trust in other things—such as health, wealth, rank, abilities, or family—rather than in God. In what areas of your life are you tempted to say, "God, I've got this covered"?

2. Can you identify other birthmarks or blemishes that prevent Jesus' light from penetrating your life?

3. The blemish of "self" blocks the light of Christ in your life. Ask God to help you identify specific instances in the past week where you may have been selfish. Ask God to forgive you.

4. The rich young ruler (Mark 10:17-27 and Luke 18:18-27) placed his security in land and riches. How did Jesus' command to sell his possessions and give the money to the poor address his flaw of misplaced faith? What might Jesus be telling you to do with the items identified in Question 1? If you doubt or feel any reluctance to being obedient, stop and ask God to give you a willing heart and increased faith.

5. Memorize Philippians 2:3. These are words you want imprinted forever on your mind! How can memorizing this verse help you guard against the blemish of "self"?

6. Read James 5:16. We are told as Christians to confess our sins, not for our salvation but for healing. What sins do you need to confess? Who would be a safe person to listen and pray with you?

CHAPTER 5

1. What is the single biggest concern in your life? Write it down or share it with a trusted person.

2. In what ways do you currently question God? His promises? His character? His actions? Do you believe that God cherishes you specifically? If so, why? If not, why not?

3. Jana shared three ways her childhood wounds and encounters with evil created "fissures" in her faith. Pray and ask God to strengthen your faith and to heal your own fractures from the past.

4. Read Hebrews 11:1. Rewrite the verse as it relates to your life.

5. Write down seven words that describe God's character. How have you seen Him display these qualities?

6. Read Philippians 4:4-9. What does Paul tell us to do in verse 4? What does he say *not* to do in verse 6? In verse 7, what does he say happens when we follow his advice? What does he tell his readers to "think on" or "meditate about" in verse 8?

CHAPTER 6

1. We use the word "*kazaap!*" to define a moment in which something is instantaneously changed into something entirely different. Have you ever been changed because of a *kazaap!* in your relationship with God? What were the circumstances that set up the moment? What happened? How were you different following your *kazaap*!

2. Have you experienced an event where something happened beyond your power and you knew it was God? How did you respond?

3. Do you have assurance that the Holy Spirit dwells within you and empowers you? What do you learn about the Holy

Spirit in these verses: John 14:16, 17; Acts 4:31; Romans 8:26, 27; 1 Corinthians 12:7-11; Galatians 5:22; and Hebrews 2:4?

4. In what ways does the Holy Spirit equip you? Empower you? Train you? Are there other forms of service that you sense a desire to fulfill? Pray and ask for specific ways to empower, equip, or bless others.

CHAPTER 7

1. Consider your parents, grandparents, and great grandparents. Describe one negative belief or action that has been passed down to you that you want to avoid. Describe one belief or action you want to embrace. What legacy do you desire to leave for future generations?

2. List three attitudes or emotions you want to release in your life so you can walk unhindered with God.

3. One of Jenny's favorite places to visit was the mall. After her death we struggled with shopping or even entering a mall. Sometimes our daily walk is challenged by memories of places or things of the past. We had to reclaim those places and memories. We conquered and reclaimed the memories by creating new ones at the mall with our grandchildren. What memories hinder your daily walk? How can you reclaim these sacred grounds?

4. Write out Micah 6:8 and circle what the Lord requires. How are these "requirements" being revealed in your life? Which of these qualities would you ask God to develop?

5. What about your life feels routine, repetitive, and monotonous? Are you frustrated by these duties or do you see value in them? Explain. In what way is God grinding away your selfish desires in order to better reflect His glory?

6. How does God teach or show you personally the way to walk? (Psalm 119:45; Psalm 143:8; Proverbs 2:7; Isaiah 30:21)

CHAPTER 8

1. Make two columns on a sheet of paper. In one column list the situations that have caused you to scream, "Why God?" In the second column, across from each situation, write any benefit you may have learned in that time of testing.

2. Put the letter "S" by every situation you have fully surrendered to God and the letter "U" by those situations you are struggling to fully give to Him. Spend time in prayer for each "U" that you marked and ask God to help you fully surrender those situations to Him.

3. Read 2 Chronicles 20:5, 6; 10-12; 20-24; 2 Kings 19:10-20 and 32-36. According to these verses, why can you feel confident surrendering all things to God?

4. Scripture says that God sometimes tests us in order to purify us. Consider a time when God tested you. Read Malachi 3:2 and Zechariah 13:9. Testing means to purify or purge away. With this definition, what benefits often come as a result of being tested or refined?

CHAPTER 9

1. Reflect upon a time in which you suffered deeply. Did this suffering cause you to doubt God's character or His justice? If so, how?

2. Does the idea that God has all things under control comfort you or disturb you? Explain.

3. In the book of Job we are invited into God's "throne room" where we witness a few "behind the scenes" conversations between God and Satan (Job 1:6-12; 2:1-7). List the attributes of God that you learn from this meeting.

4. List the attributes of Satan that are revealed in this same meeting.

5. What differences do you see between the authority and character of God and of Satan?

6. Look up the words *correct* and *condemn* in the dictionary. Read Proverbs 3:11, 12; John 8:10, 11; and Revelation 12:10. Who corrects us and why? Who condemns us and why? Think about a person who has suffered greatly because someone else has slandered or violated them and they've seen no justice—their "enemy" has escaped with no apparent consequences. Read Deuteronomy 32:35; Job 34:11, 12; Prov. 11:21; and Romans 12:19. What hope do these verses offer when justice appears to be absent?

CHAPTER 10

1. If your faith has ever been shaken, did God intervene in some unexpected way to encourage or restore your hope? If so, describe the event. If not, and you feel your faith is weak, pray and ask God for help and patience.

2. Why do you think God personally intervened to "lift Job's face" after he had suffered so many losses (Job 42:9)?

3. Hope and faith are inextricably linked. Hebrews 11:1 teaches that faith is the assurance of things you hope for. What does this verse suggest about your faith when all hope has been lost?

4. Read Romans 10:17. According to this verse, how can faith be restored?

5. Read Job 42:7-10. God said twice to Eliphaz: "...you have not spoken of Me what is right, as My servant Job has." What do you think God saw in Job's heart that was right? What did He observe in Eliphaz's heart that was wrong? Later it says that God "lifted Job's face" (or "accepted Job"). Do you think that God used Eliphaz in this process? If so, how?

6. In Romans 10:17 the Greek meaning for "Word" in this passage is "rhema," which emphasizes the spoken Word of God. Why do you suppose the spoken Word is emphasized? Pray and ask the Father to give you a specific Word that will "perfect, confirm, strengthen, and establish you" (1 Peter 5:10).

7. Is God leading you to speak to another who has lost hope? Send that person a gift, a text, or a note of encouragement, or call and offer to pray together. Listening and praying are two concrete ways to love another person.

CHAPTER 11

1. Can you recall a time when God "lifted your face"—when it seemed as if He put His finger beneath your chin, tilted your face upwards, and affirmed you? How did the infilling of His tenderness, love, and mercy change you?

2. Write the H.O.P.E. acronym on a piece of paper. Think about a challenging situation you are in or one you recently experienced. Where are you in the acronym? How does the H.O.P.E. acronym change your perspective in your current pain or crisis?

3. What are different ways you can celebrate or make new memories for the anniversary dates that represent a great loss?

4. Do you know someone who is facing devastating circumstances? According to the H.O.P.E. acronym, how might you be able to offer encouragement?

5. Memorize one or both of these Scriptures:

   "…and hope does not disappoint, because the love of God has been poured out within our hearts through the Holy Spirit who was given to us" (Romans 5:5).

"Now may the God of hope fill you with all joy and peace in believing, so that you will abound in hope by the power of the Holy Spirit" (Romans 15:13).

Endnotes

CHAPTER 1
[1] 1 Peter 2:4, 5
[2] John Piper, *Don't Waste Your Life*, (Wheaton, IL: Crosswalk Books. 2003), p. 73.
[3] Ephesians 1:18
[4] Paraphrase of Mark 14:36

CHAPTER 2
[1] Genesis 3:1-6
[2] C.S. Lewis, *The Problem of Pain* (New York, NY: HarperCollins Publishers, 1996), pp. 77, 79.
[3] Exodus 33:18-23
[4] Andrew Murray, *The Practice of God's Presence, Seven-in-One Anthology*, (New Kensington, PA: Whitaker House, 2000), p. 308.
[5] R.C. Sproul, "Cosmic Treason," Tabletalk, (May 2008), p. 7.

CHAPTER 3
[1] Frequent quote by Sr. Pastor Dan Carroll, Water of Life Community Church; Fontana, CA.
[2] John 8:39, 41, 52, 53
[3] John 7:41, 42, 51, 52
[4] John 3:4
[5] John 3:14, 15
[6] Psalm 2
[7] John 3:19
[8] John 3:21

9 John 4:10
10 Paraphrase of John 4:17, 18
11 Paraphrase of John 4:23, 24
12 Paraphrase of John 4:26
13 John 1:9
14 Matthew 5:14
15 Matthew 5:16
16 C. H. Spurgeon, "Light at Evening Time," The Spurgeon Archive #3508, (April 20, 1916).

CHAPTER 4

1 Ephesians 2:10
2 Revelation 1:14, 16
3 Revelation 2:18
4 Revelation 2:19
5 Revelation 2:20
6 Revelation 2:23
7 Mark 10:17-27; Luke 18:18-27
8 Mark 10:17
9 Mark 10:18
10 Mark 10:19
11 Mark 10:20
12 Mark 10:21
13 Mark 10:21
14 Mark 10:22
15 Matthew 26:31
16 Matthew 26:33, 35
17 Mark 14:27-30; Luke 22:31-34
18 Mark 14:66-70
19 Mark 14:71
20 Mark 14:66-72; Luke 22:55-62
21 Andrew Murray, *Absolute Surrender*, (Online, Unlisted Address: Feather Trail Press, 2010), p. 37.

ENDNOTES

CHAPTER 5

[1] C. S. Lewis, *A Grief Observed*, (San Francisco, CA: Harper San Francisco, 2001), pp. 22, 23.

CHAPTER 6

[1] Kay Arthur, Precept Upon Precept Bible Study.
[2] Genesis 17:11
[3] Genesis 17
[4] Leviticus 26:12
[5] Hebrews 8:6
[6] Zechariah 7:12
[7] Deuteronomy 10:12-16
[8] Ezekiel 11:19, 20
[9] Hebrews 9:15 (NIV)
[10] Gemological Institute of America, Gem Encyclopedia Web site: http://www.gia.edu/emerald
[11] Keller, P. C. "Emeralds of Columbia," Gems and Gemology; Summer, 1981, pp. 80-92.
[12] Genesis 9:13-16
[13] Acts 1:4, 5, 8
[14] Charles Stanley, *The Wonderful Spirit Filled Life*, (Nashville, TN: Thomas Nelson Publishers, 1992), p. 16.
[15] Deuteronomy 30:6; Philippians 3:3; Colossians 2:11
[16] 1 Corinthians 12:4-11
[17] John 16:13
[18] Pastor Rolo Santos, Water of Life Church; Fontana, CA.
[19] Dennis McCallum, "A Chronological Study of Paul's Ministry," online article (Columbus, OH: Xenos Christian Fellowship, 2012); http://www.xenos.org/classes/chronop.htm
[20] Philippians 3:6; Acts 9:1
[21] Acts 7:54-60
[22] Acts 9:1-6

23 Acts 9:8, 9
24 Acts 9:10-18
25 Galatians 6:17
26 Charles Stanley, *The Wonderful Spirit Filled Life*, (Nashville, TN: Thomas Nelson Publishers, 1992), p. 47.

CHAPTER 7

1. William Gaultiere, Ph.D. is the Director of New Hope Crisis Counseling at the Crystal Cathedral and a Psychologist with ChristianSoulCare.com. http://www.newhopenow.org/selfhelp/dependent.adrenaline.html referenced 6/27/2014.
2. B. Ganzel, B.J. Casey, G. Glover, H.U. Voss, E. Temple, "The Aftermath of 9/11: Effect of Intensity and Regency of Trauma on Outcome," Emotion, (Vol. 7, No. 2, 2007; by the American Psychological Association) pp. 227-238; http://www.apa.org/pubs/journals/releases/emo-72227.pdf
3. D.H. Barlow and V.M. Durand. "Chapter Two/Section/ Neuroscience and Its Contributions to Psychopathology," Abnormal Psychology: An Integrative Approach (Belmont, CA: Wadsworth, 2005), pp. 30-67.
4. A. Hart, "Addiction & Recovery" Adrenaline Addiction, Lesson 16, DVD, 2009; www.lightuniversity.com
5. Senior Pastor Steve Holsinger, Faith Christian Community; Anchorage, AK.
6. Oswald Chambers, "Dependent on God's Presence," in My Utmost for His Highest Daily Devotional Journal, (Uhrichsville, OH: Barbour Pub, 2010), p. July 20th.

CHAPTER 8

1. Matthew 27:44
2. Luke 23:40-42
3. Luke 23:43

4. Mark 5:22, 23
5. Mark 5:35
6. Mark 5:36
7. Mark 5:35-43
8. Romans 5:11
9. Romans 5:5

CHAPTER 9

1. Jeremiah 29:11
2. Isaiah 55:9
3. Charles Spurgeon, "Unconditional Surrender," Sermon #1276, Metropolitan Tabernacle Pulpit, Jan. 30, 1876, Vol. 22; www.spurgeongems.org
4. Thomas Merton, *New Seeds of Contemplation*, (New York, NY: New Directions Publishing Corporation, 1961)
5. Andrew Murray, *Absolute Surrender*, (Online, Unlisted Address: Feather Trail Press, 2010), p. 7.
6. George Barna, *Maximum Faith*, (Austin, TX: Fedd and Company, Inc., 2011), p. 22.
7. Job 1:8
8. Job 1:9, 10
9. Job 1:12
10. Job 1:13-22
11. Job 1:21
12. Job 1:22
13. Job 2:4, 5
14. Job 2:10
15. Job 4:8
16. Job 8:6
17. Job 11:13, 15
18. Job 6:14
19. Job 16:4, 5 (NLT)

[20] Job 10:2, 3; 19:6, 7
[21] Job 23:3-6; 31:6
[22] Job 31:35
[23] Job 38, 39 (assorted verses)
[24] Paraphrase of Job 38:16, 19, 35
[25] Job 40:4, 5
[26] Job 42:1-6
[27] Galatians 6:1
[28] 2 Corinthians 1:4

CHAPTER 10

[1] Ravi Zacharias, *Cries of the Heart*; (Nashville, TN: Thomas Nelson Publishers, 1997) p. 89.
[2] John 4:28
[3] John 4:29-42
[4] John 4:39
[5] Daniel 6:16-24
[6] Daniel 9:16
[7] Daniel 9:20-23
[8] John 3:14, 15
[9] John 3:19
[10] John 11:50
[11] Romans 15:1, 2
[12] Henri J.M. Nouwen, *Life of the Beloved: Spiritual Living in a Secular World*, (New York: Crossroad Publishing, 1992) p. 97.

CHAPTER 11

[1] The setting that won the competition was "Embracing Hope." The Hope Diamond was mounted in the platinum setting and necklace, accompanied by 340 baguette diamonds.
[2] http://alohaisles.com/bigisland/geography.htm

3. Casting Crowns. *Who Am I*. Rec. Feb. 2004. Mark A. Miller, Steven Curtis Chapman.
4. Psalm 42:5
5. http://www.beliefnet.com/Quotes/Christian/C/Catherine-Marshall/God-Is-The-Only-One-Who-Can-Make-The-Valley-Of-Tro.aspx retrieved 7/21/2004.
6. Guthrie, Nancy. *Holding on to Hope: A Pathway through Suffering to the Heart of God*. (p. 100) Wheaton, IL: Tyndale House, 2002. Print.
7. http://www.intouch.org/magazine/content.aspx?topic=What_is_Hope#.U8Sa7U1OVjo retrieved 7/14/14.
8. Psalm 22
9. Guthrie, Nancy. *Holding on to Hope: A Pathway through Suffering to the Heart of God*. (p. 98) Wheaton, IL: Tyndale House, 2002. Print.
10. Wilson, Rod. *How Do I Help a Hurting Friend?* Grand Rapids, MI: Baker, 2006. 64. Print.
11. Chang, Valerie Nash., Sheryn Thompson. Scott, and Carol L. Decker. *Developing Helping Skills: A Step-by-step Approach*. Belmont, CA: Brooks/Cole Cengage Learning, 2009. 83-89. Print.
12. Chang, Valerie Nash., Sheryn Thompson. Scott, and Carol L. Decker. *Developing Helping Skills: A Step-by-step Approach*. Belmont, CA: Brooks/Cole Cengage Learning, 2009. 132-135. Print.
13. Philippians 4:4-9 (ESV)
14. Romans 5:3-5
15. Wright, H. Norman. *Helping Those Who Hurt*. Minneapolis, MN: Bethany House, 2003. 96-97. Print.